David Livingstone

and the Rovuma

A NOTEBOOK

edited with *Introduction* and
related documents by

GEORGE SHEPPERSON

Professor of Commonwealth History
University of Edinburgh

Edinburgh
at the University Press

© GEORGE SHEPPERSON 1965
EDINBURGH UNIVERSITY PRESS
George Square, Edinburgh 8
North America
Aldine Publishing Company
320 West Adams Street, Chicago
Australia and New Zealand
Hodder & Stoughton Limited
Africa, Oxford University Press
India, P. C. Manaktala & Sons
Far East, M. Graham Brash & Son

Printed in Great Britain
by T. & A. Constable Ltd., Hopetoun Street
Printers to the University of Edinburgh

Contents

Abbreviations

It is hoped that this list will not only save the reader much unnecessary scanning of print but will also serve as a bibliographical guide to the student who wishes to discover more of Livingstone's East and Central African projects.

B William Garden Blaikie,
The Personal Life of David Livingstone
(London, 1880).

cha Owen Chadwick,
Mackenzie's Grave
(London, 1959).

cou Reginald Coupland,
Kirk on the Zambesi
(Oxford, 1928).

D Frank Debenham,
The Way to Ilala. David Livingstone's Pilgrimage
(London, 1955).

KZJ Kirk's Zambezi journal.
(The manuscript of this is in the possession of Mrs R. Foskett. By the time this book appears, it is hoped that Mr R. Foskett's edition of the manuscript, under the title of *The Zambesi Journal of Dr. John Kirk*, will have been published.)

LJ *The Last Journals of David Livingstone in Central Africa, from 1865 to his death,*
edited by Horace Waller (London, 1874),
Volume I.

LMB Livingstone Memorial, Blantyre, Lanarkshire, Scotland.

NLS National Library of Scotland, Edinburgh.

R Mrs Charles E. Russell,
General Rigby, Zanzibar and the Slave Trade
(London, 1935).

RGSJ *Journal of the Royal Geographical Society*
(London).

RGSP *Proceedings of the Royal Geographical Society*
     (London).
S   George Seaver,
     David Livingstone
     (London, 1957).
ZEDL *The Zambezi Expedition of David Livingstone,*
     1858-1863,
     edited by J. P. R. Wallis
     (London, 1956), two volumes.
ZJJS *The Zambezi Journal of James Stewart, 1862-1863*
     (London, 1952).
ZT   David and Charles Livingstone,
     Narrative of an Expedition to the Zambesi
     and its Tributaries ... 1858-1864
     (London, 1865).

Spelling and Pronunciation

In the period of European exploration and occupation of East and Central Africa, words in the African languages were spelt in a confusing variety of ways by the early pioneers of the Partition. In this book, I have attempted to follow the more generally accepted modern usages—except in those instances where there is a possibility of their confusing the reader—in the introductory essay and in the explanatory notes to the documents. In the documents themselves, however, unless otherwise stated, I have retained the original spellings. This may mean that a word is sometimes spelt in one way in the quotations from documents and in another in the introductory essay and explanatory notes: for example, *Zambesi* and *Zambezi*, *Nyassa* and *Nyasa*, *Quillimane* and *Quelimane*, *Tette* and *Tete*, *Pomone* and *Pomony*. But the variations of such spellings are usually so slight that the reader should have no difficulty in following them.

In one case, however, I have departed from my general rule. This is in the spelling of *Rovuma*. The modern spelling is *Ruvuma*. As this is still not widely accepted outside East Africa (for example, the 1962 edition of the *Encyclopaedia Britannica* uses Rovuma), I have employed throughout this book the original spelling by David Livingstone and others of *Rovuma*. I have also used throughout the expression *Comoro Islands* rather than the *Archipel des Comores* which is now appearing in many atlases.

All African words are to be pronounced on the general Bantu pattern, stressing the penultimate syllable. There are no silent letters and every syllable is open. The vowels have the Italian values as in '*Il* Tr*ovatore* by Gi*u*s*e*ppe Verd*i*'. *l* and *r* are used interchangeably, although *l* tends to displace *r* in modern spelling. *m* or *n* at the start of a word and before another consonant is lightly pronounced as a rule.

Acknowledgements

I am indebted to the Librarian of the National Library of
Scotland for permission to consult Livingstone's 1862
Rovuma field notebook and other relevant documents
and to reproduce the field notebook; to the Warden of
the Livingstone Memorial, Blantyre, Scotland, for allow-
ing me to examine documents and the *Orestes* logbook,
portions of which he permitted me to print; to Mrs R.
Foskett, granddaughter of Sir John Kirk, for permission
to quote from his Zambezi journal; to Mr David Mc-
Master for helpful advice on maps; and to Mr Thomas
Price for generous comments on the introductory essay
and some other parts of this book. In particular, I wish to
express my gratitude to Mr A. R. Turnbull, Secretary to
the Edinburgh University Press, and to Miss Jenifer
Marshall, of the Press Staff, for providing a preliminary
transcription of the major part of the Rovuma field notebook and for giving me friendly encouragement and criticism, without which I might have got stuck beyond extri-
cation in the literary mangrove forests which impede the
interpreter of Livingstone's notes on the Rovuma almost
as much as the actual forests of that resistant river prevented the progress of the great explorer himself.

George Shepperson

David Livingstone and the Rovuma

AN INTRODUCTORY ESSAY

Dr Livingstone is unquestionably a traveller of talents, enterprise, and excellent constitution, but it is now plain enough that his zeal and imagination much surpass his judgement.

(*Quoted in* The Times, *London, 20 January 1863*)

1

THE HERO

David Livingstone was the victim of his own early successes. In 1840, at the age of twenty-seven, he had gone out to southern Africa as an unknown missionary of humble social origins. He came home again in 1856, after a journey of four years in the centre of Africa to parts where few white men had ventured. He had crossed the continent from east to west and visited the 'thundering smoke' of the great rush of waters from the Zambesi which he named the Victoria Falls. It was a journey that caught the imagination of men on both sides of the Atlantic, ignorant of Africa and avid for sensational news of what they liked to call the 'Dark Continent'; towards which a volatile mixture of science and speculation, conscience and commerce, religion and religiosity, was increasingly turning their attention. The mid-nineteenth century public was ready for a hero such as David Livingstone.

From lecture platform to missionary meeting, he toured Britain, telling of his adventures and outlining his schemes for the 'redemption' of Africa by the abolition of the Arab and Portuguese slave trade and by the uplifting of the indigenous inhabitants through a programme of Victorian Christianity, capitalism and colonization. Honours flowed in upon him; and when his account of the journey, *Missionary Travels and Researches in South Africa*, was scheduled for publication at the end of 1857 at a guinea a volume, the first edition of twelve thousand copies was over-subscribed before publication. Well might it be said in the language of the newspapers and magazines that fell upon his every word and carried it to a rapidly-growing reading public that he had the whole of Britain 'at his feet'. A sequel to Livingstone's travels, on foot and in print, was inevitable. But a journey like that of 1852-6, alone and relatively unaided and 'epoch-making' in all senses of that much-abused phrase, could not be repeated. Furthermore, such a public mood of over-confidence in Livingstone was bound to result in anti-climax.

Statesmen as well as simple sensation-seekers responded to Livingstone's plans for a new African journey. Early in 1857 he had an interview with the Foreign Secretary, Lord Clarendon. 'Just come here and tell me what you want,' Clarendon had said to him, 'and I will give it to you.' The Prime Minister, Palmerston, was an old anti-slavery *aficionado*, and took a personal interest in Livingstone's plans. The result was that, on 8 February 1858, Livingstone was appointed British Consul at Quelimane, the Portuguese East African port, 'for the Eastern Coast and independent districts of the interior, and commander of an expedition for exploring Eastern and Central Africa, for the promotion of Commerce and Civilization with a view to the extinction of the slave trade'. He was given a steamship, a free hand to choose the personnel of his expedition, £5,000 worth of equipment and a salary five times as much as he had received when an employee of the London Missionary Society. On 13 February he went to Buckingham Palace for a private interview with the Queen; attended a farewell banquet at the Freemasons Tavern at which three hundred and fifty distinguished guests were present; and, four weeks later, was on his way again to Africa. The anti-climax had begun.

The years of Livingstone's Zambezi Expedition, 1858-1864, were a compound of bathos, pathos and genuine achievement. The bathos and pathos have often been chronicled and criticized: Livingstone's quarrels with the members of the expedition; his obstinately uncritical support of his awkward, if not 'malevolent'[1] brother, Charles, who had left the pastorate of a church in the United States where he had studied theology, to accompany the expedition to which, whether for reasons of health or simply through weakness of character,[2] he brought so much discord; Livingstone's exaggerated economic expectations; the fiasco of the first Universities Mission to Central Africa (the result of Livingstone's moving appeal in the Senate House, Cambridge, in 1857) which was sent out to join him three years later and most of whose leading members were dead in little over twelve months; and, above all, the death of his wife, Mary, who came to Livingstone on the Zambezi in February 1862, and died there within three months. It is a melancholy record. And not even the genuine achievements have been left untarnished. Livingstone's idea for an 'English colony'[3]—Scotland's national hero avoided 'British'[4]—in Nyasaland has been criticized by Malawi nationalists; and his 'discovery' of Lake Nyasa on 16 September 1859 has been held up to scorn by one of their ministers on the grounds that the Lake 'had already been known by our people for years'.[5]

Of this melancholy chronicle, as the words from the London *Times* of 1863 at the start of this essay indicate, one of the most miserable elements, at first sight, was Livingstone's passion for the reluctant Rovuma.

[1] D, p. 150.
[2] Compare s, pp. 303-4: 'His behaviour on the Expedition seems strangely out of keeping with his previous and also his subsequent career.'
[3] s, p. 308.
[4] See George Shepperson, 'David Livingstone the Scot,' *Scottish Historical Review* (Edinburgh), XXXIX, 1960, p. 112.
[5] *Malawi News* (Limbe), Vol. 5, No. 111, 15 March 1963, p. 3.

2
POLITICS AND ECONOMICS

Even today, the Rovuma river is little more than a name
—if that—to most people. Almost five hundred miles
long in its entire complicated course, it forms the boundary between Tanganyika and Portuguese East Africa: a
natural line of political partition which goes back to the
settlement of 1886 when the southern extremities of German East Africa (as Tanganyika was then called) were
demarcated. The Rovuma was strategically important
during the British conflict with the armies of General von
Lettow-Vorbeck whose crossing and re-crossing of the
river between 1916 and 1918 received some attention
from a British press that was, however, largely devoted to
events on the Western Front in Europe. The Portuguese,
certainly, do not forget the Rovuma: to them it is an
'important and historical river'[1] for the disputed territory
at whose mouth they fought an unhappy but ultimately
successful campaign against the Germans during the
First World War. But, in spite of the renewed interest
in the 1914-18 War and in the Portuguese colonies, the
Rovuma today, outside of Africa, is almost an unknown
river.

David Livingstone, too, knew little about it at first. Yet
his interest in it was a practical one: it was a 'river ex-
terior to Portuguese claims', as he put it.[2] When preparations were being made for the Zambezi Expedition,
Livingstone had been worried about these claims. His
crossing of Africa on his great journey of 1852-6 had
taught him something of Portuguese power in the hinterland which, although it was ill-supported by soldiers on
the spot, had three centuries of Lusitanian imperialism

[1] *Grande Enciclopédia Portugesa e Brasileira* (Lisbon,
1945), XXVI, columns 310-17.

[2] B, p. 279; J. P. R. Wallis, editor, *The Matebele Mission*
(London, 1945), p. 310.

16

behind it. This imperialism may have seemed half-awake for at least a hundred and fifty years. But it was evidently a light sleeper: for, although the Portuguese Government had received the overtures of the British Foreign Office about Livingstone's expedition in a friendly manner, it had been stirred to action again and had taken the precaution, on 4 February 1858, of making a public reassertion of its sovereignty over the Zambezi area, the waterway to the slaving preserves of Central Africa which it was Livingstone's ambition to destroy. And when, by September 1859, Livingstone had found in the highlands at the southern end of Lake Nyasa a desirable spot for a British colony that could be reached by the Shire river from the Zambezi, he had another reason for being irked by Portuguese claims.

Livingstone was later to write

The Portuguese Government had refused to open the Zambesi to the ships of other nations, and their officials were very effectually pursuing a system, which by abstracting the labour, was rendering the country of no value either to foreigners or to themselves.[1]

To drive the point home, the Portuguese increased their installations on the Zambezi. Livingstone was to sum up his feelings about these moves in a letter to the British Consul at Zanzibar early in 1862. He complained that the Portuguese had

built a fort lately at the mouth of the Shire, and put up a custom house at Kongone, the mouth of the Zambesi, we discovered, as a claim to dues when the cotton trade shall be discovered; and the Governor of Tette [a Portuguese settlement, three hundred miles up the Zambezi] does all he can to depopulate the country from which the cotton comes by slave-hunting.[2]

The references to cotton indicate another of Livingstone's reasons for wanting an alternative river route into East and Central Africa. In 1857 he had visited Man-

---

[1] ZT, p. 348.   [2] R, p. 228.

chester, the centre of the British cotton goods industry, and had been welcomed by its Chamber of Commerce, whose appetite was whetted by what he had to tell them of cotton-growing and other commercial possibilities in Central Africa. It passed a 'very cordial resolution'[1] supporting his schemes for developing the region. This encouraged Livingstone to keep his eyes open for potential cotton-growing areas during the Zambezi Expedition: not that he needed much encouragement, since with the background of his work as a young man in the Blantyre Mill, Scotland, as a cotton-piecer, and with his anti-slavery animus driving him on to find for British industry alternative sources of cotton to those provided by the plantations of the slave-ridden South in the United States, he never let slip an opportunity to survey the possibilities for cotton of any promising piece of African ground. Such a promising piece, with Africans accustomed to cotton cultivation, Livingstone believed he had discovered in the Lake Nyasa regions. He wrote

Three varieties of cotton are to be found in the country, namely, two foreign and one native. The tonge manga, or foreign cotton, the name showing that it has been introduced, is of excellent quality, and considered by Manchester to be nearly equal to the best New Orleans.[2]

The Portuguese may have introduced these seeds but, so far as Livingstone was concerned, their commercial restrictions, slave-raiding and archaic methods of production were holding back its large-scale cultivation. An alternative route, therefore, into what Livingstone claimed, exaggeratedly as time would show, was potentially rich cotton country, was urgently needed. It was imperative, he considered, 'to see whether the River Rovuma will serve us as an outlet to a cotton field 300 miles long which we have examined'.[3]

[1] B, p. 218.

[2] ZT, p. 111.

[3] NLS: Acc. 662, Livingstone from *Pioneer*, 22 February 1862. Compare ZEDL, p. 342.

The Rovuma, forty-five miles of which were already known,[1] was the only other river on the east coast of Africa that seemed likely to provide this alternative route. As early as December 1859,[2] if not earlier, the idea had occurred to Livingstone; and he had written to the British Government about it and had received a reply approving his plans to reach Lake Nyasa by way of the Rovuma. The same mail brought him the information that the *Pioneer*, the new and more powerful vessel for which he had asked, was on its way. It also carried the news that a large party of missionaries, led by the recently consecrated Anglican Bishop, Charles Frederick Mackenzie, was coming out to establish the Universities Mission to Central Africa in the Zambezi regions, and expected Livingstone's help. This was an additional complication.

3

THE FIRST ATTEMPT

On 7 February 1861, Bishop Mackenzie and his party were at the Kongone mouth of the Zambezi. Livingstone was waiting for them. But, as the historian of Mackenzie's venture writes,

The Bishop landed at the Kongone intending to take his mission up the Zambezi. Livingstone sailed down the Zambezi to the Kongone intending to take himself and the mission to the Rovuma.[3]

Livingstone's intention to take the missionaries with him up the Rovuma was no part of a policy to show them more of Africa. His Rovuma exploration was already delayed. Livingstone had promised the Makololo, some of whom he had taken with him on his expeditions northward and had left at Tete, that he would see that they got safely home again. These were a people whom he had met on his first African journey, in what is now Bechuana-

[1] B, p. 279.   [2] ZEDL, pp. 343-5.   [3] Cha, p. 30.

land. So he had kept this promise to them, and this had taken up, in 1860, months which he could otherwise have spent in an attempt on the Rovuma. The attempt was further delayed by the *Pioneer's* two months' lateness in arriving. The river, moreover, was in flood. The Portuguese, too, had got word of Livingstone's schemes. The Governor-General of Portuguese East Africa had rushed up to see the Sultan of Zanzibar in the hope that he would agree to the Rovuma as the boundary between his territories on the mainland and those of the Portuguese.[1] Speed and secrecy were therefore, Livingstone believed, essential for his plans. On 17 August 1860, he had written to Thomas Maclear, the Astronomer Royal at the Cape, 'We go to the Rovuma to try to find an entrance away from the Portuguese. But this we do not tell everyone.'[2] With an old college friend in Scotland, James Young, he had been more explicit: 'We keep our movements secret from the Portuguese—and so must you; they seize everything they see in the newspapers. Who are my imprudent friends who publicize everything?'[3] At the best of times, Livingstone was a stubborn man; but, with these considerations in mind, he was in no mood to argue with Bishop Mackenzie about whose journey should have priority. It was obvious to Livingstone that his should have it.

Mackenzie, therefore, acceded to Livingstone's proposal that he should join him, his brother Charles, and the young Edinburgh doctor, John Kirk, the Expedition's botanist, in the *Pioneer* for an exploration of the Rovuma. The rest of the Bishop's party were to wait for them at Johanna, a British naval station and one of the Comoro group of islands (called today Anjouan) at which there was a British Consulate, that lay off the east African coast between Cape Delgado and Madagascar.

Livingstone and the other Rovuma explorers went ahead of Mackenzie to the river and, while waiting for him, took

[1] R, p. 228.
[2] LMB, Sesheke, 17 August 1800.
[3] B, p. 279. See also R, p. 227.

20

the opportunity of examining its mouths. There seemed no bar in its broad and deep main channel as it issued into a bay which could provide safe anchorage for ships. The land rose to some three hundred feet about eight miles upstream. This suggested that the Rovuma might offer a speedier passage than the Zambezi, through the fever-breeding flats. In fact, it seemed likely to be a considerable improvement on the Portuguese river.

On 12 March 1861,[1] after three days of argument between Livingstone and Mackenzie, the little party in the *Pioneer* set off for David Livingstone's first essay with the Rovuma. But after getting only thirty miles upstream, they turned back. The return was difficult, with the *Pioneer* going aground frequently. Had the river not been gradually rising, Livingstone believed that they would have remained aground for a whole season. The hard work which was demanded of all of them drove his arguments with Mackenzie out of his mind and he noted in his journal that 'Bishop worked very hard in boats the whole time, an excellent fellow'.[2] On 23 March, a fortnight after setting out, the *Pioneer* was back at the mouth of the Rovuma. Livingstone's hopes had not been realized.

He later wrote a laconic account of this episode:

We proceeded up the river, and saw that it had fallen four or five feet during our detention. The scenery on the lower part of the Rovuma is superior to that on the Zambesi, for we can see the highlands from the sea. Eight miles from the mouth the mangroves are left behind, and a beautiful range of well-wooded hills on each bank begins. On these ridges the tree resembling African blackwood, of finer grain than ebony, grows abundantly, and attains a large size. Few people were seen, and those of Arab breed, and did not appear to be very well off. The current of the Rovuma was now as strong as that of the Zambesi, but the volume of water is very much less. Several of the crossings

[1] cha, p. 30; ZT, p. 349, gives 11 March.
[2] ZEDL, p. 178.

had barely water enough for our ship, drawing five feet, to pass. When we were thirty miles up the river, the water fell suddenly seven inches in twenty-four hours. As the March flood is the last of the season, and it appeared to be expended, it was thought prudent to avoid the chance of a year's detention, by getting the ship back to the sea without delay. Had the Expedition been alone, we would have pushed up in boats, or afoot, and done what we could towards the exploration of the river and the upper end of the lake; but, though the Mission was a private one, and entirely distinct from our own, the objects of both being similar, we felt anxious to aid our countrymen in their noble enterprise; and, rather than follow our own inclination, decided to return to the Shire, see the Mission party settled safely, and afterwards explore Lake Nyassa and the Rovuma from the Lake downwards. Fever broke out on board the *Pioneer*, at the mouth of the Rovuma, as we thought from our having anchored close to a creek coming out of mangroves; and it remained in her until we completely isolated the engine-room from the rest of the ship. The coal dust rotting sent out strong effluvia, and kept up the disease for more than a twelvemonth.[1]

John Kirk was less laconic about the Rovuma's mangroves. He wrote in melodramatic terms about the 'maritime vegetation' at its mouth:

dark, gloomy and damp mangrove forests, loaded with malaria and swarming with mosquitoes, where the sun seldom pierces through the leaves above and a death-like stillness prevails, broken only by the wild scream of some fish-eagle or the chatter of the monkey.[2]

In his more sober account, Livingstone mentioned that 'several of the crossings had barely enough water for our ship, drawing five feet, to pass'. He did not mention one of the main reasons for this: that the extra ballast which had been put into the *Pioneer* to enable her to face up to the voyage from Britain had increased her draught

[1] ZT, pp. 349-50.   [2] RGSJ, XXXV, 1865, p. 155.

from the designed three feet to five.[1] Indeed, the senior British naval officer off the Kongone mouth of the Zambezi had pointed out that the Rovuma was only navigable for most of its course in boats. In his next expedition up the Rovuma, in 1862, Livingstone clearly benefited from his journey of 1861 by making the ascent in a couple of boats. The subject was obviously on his mind as the *Pioneer* went back to Johanna to pick up the other missionaries and return them all to the Zambezi, for on 9 April 1861 he wrote to the Royal Geographical Society in London that the Rovuma 'must be navigated with a vessel of light draught and with the same skill as is required in the above-bridge London passenger-boats'.[2]

He gained further naval experience on his way back to the Zambezi as a result of the fever that broke out among the unseasoned Europeans on the *Pioneer*, only four out of twenty of whom escaped it.[3] Livingstone was forced to navigate the vessel for long periods by himself. As Professor Frank Debenham, whose study of Livingstone as a geographer is a turning-point in the appreciation of his Rovuma ventures, says, the 'excursion had brought Livingstone out in a new light, as a ship-master'.[4] It was an experience which stood him in good stead at the end of the Zambezi Expedition when, having failed to sell the launch, *Lady Nyassa*, which had been constructed for him in Scotland in 1862 at his own expense, Livingstone was compelled to navigate her himself, with a makeshift crew, over two thousand miles across the Indian Ocean, from Zanzibar to Bombay.

Despite his increased skill in seamanship, Livingstone's first journey on the Rovuma had clearly not been a success. It could not, however, be written off as a pure fiasco. He told the Royal Geographical Society frankly that he did not believe that the river came out of Lake Nyasa, although he had acquired plenty of African testi-

[1] COU, p. 189.   [2] RGSP, VI, 1861-2, p. 20.

[3] Michael Gelfand, *Livingstone the Doctor* (Oxford, 1957), p. 304.

[4] D, p. 186.

mony that it did. Nevertheless, the Society could still accept his assertion that the Rovuma would probably turn out to be 'the best entrance into Eastern Africa'.[1]

4

THE ROVUMA FROM NYASA : A SECOND ATTEMPT

After his return to the Zambezi at the beginning of May 1861, Livingstone spent two difficult and dangerous months helping Bishop Mackenzie and his party to set up a mission station at Magomero in the Shire highlands. By August 1861, Livingstone felt free to begin again the exploration of the Lake Nyasa regions. With his brother Charles, John Kirk and an Irish seaman named John Neil and twenty African carriers, he spent a month getting a light, four-oared gig up the Shire and into Lake Nyasa. On 2 September 1861 the party entered the Lake.

The arduous two months that Livingstone spent on it did not have any one aim in view; their object was the general exploration of the 'great water' or Nyasa which Livingstone had found two years before. Nevertheless, he was determined amidst all the other problems which occupied his attention at this time to see if the rumours that the Rovuma came out of Lake Nyasa were true. In March 1861 he had tried to get into Lake Nyasa by sailing up the Rovuma. Now he would reverse the process and see if he could get into the Rovuma by sailing up Lake Nyasa. In a sense, therefore, Livingstone's venture on the Lake from 2 September to 27 October 1861 was a second Rovuma expedition.

This is clear from Livingstone's report to the Royal Geographical Society on 7 December 1861:

We have been up Lake Nyasa, and carried a boat past the cataracts to explore by. Went along the western shore; it is very deep; from 20 to 50 or 60 miles broad, and over two hundred miles long. It was excessively stormy and you must not despise us for failing to find out all about the

[1] RGSP, V, 1861-2, p. 20.

24

Rovuma. We were on the west side, and could not cross in our little boat at the period of the equinoctial gales; then we could get no food in a depopulated part of the country near the north end. Pirates live on detached rocks, and human skeletons and putrid bodies were lying everywhere. It was a fair dead lock for us and we came back.[1]

The temperamental waters of Lake Nyasa have tried many men's patience—and Livingstone, with his anxiety to skirt the claims of the Portuguese, was more than normally impatient. It is clear today that the results for geography of these two months were 'immense'.[2] But Livingstone seems to have taken little consolation from this. His remark to the Fellows of the Royal Society that 'you must not despise us for failing to find out all about the Rovuma' and his concluding cry, 'It was a fair dead lock for us' indicate despondency that he was no nearer the discovery of a route, alternative to the Zambezi, into the interior.

A similar note of dejection was struck in a letter that Livingstone had written on 1 November 1861 shortly after stowing away the frail gig, which had battled nobly but ineffectively with Lake Nyasa. It was addressed to the Secretary in Edinburgh of the Foreign Mission Board of the Free Church of Scotland, which was sending out a representative, James Stewart, to discuss with Livingstone a further mission in the Lake Nyasa regions. Livingstone apologized to the Board for the little information which he had given them about this. 'On returning from the Rovuma,' he wrote, referring to his attempt on the river in March 1861, 'I had nothing to say about it as a new missionary field and therefore no heart to write at all.' And then, with a glance at the two tumultuous months which he had just spent on Lake Nyasa, he added, 'I indulged the hope that information such as you desire might also be obtained by looking down that river from Lake Nyasa, from the attempt to do which we are now

[1] RGSJ, XXXIII, 1863, p. 251.
[2] D, p. 195.

returning'.[1] This suggests another motive for Livingstone's interest in the Rovuma: its possibilities as a field for missionary enterprise.

The conflicting testimony from dwellers on Lake Nyasa about its connections with the Rovuma was a further source of irritation for Livingstone. 'One intelligent native,' he noted, 'with apparently no motive for deceiving us, asserted most positively that our boat could sail out of the Lake into the river; another that it must be carried a few yards; while a third would maintain that the land carriage was at least fifty miles.'[2] With his wry humour, a device that often took the edge off his irritation, he commented that it was 'a good illustration of the instability of the foundations on which much speculative geography stands'.

Yet the last weeks of 1861 were not all dejection and irritation for Livingstone. His wife, from whom he had been separated for nearly four years, was coming out to join him early in the New Year. She was to travel in the steamboat, *Lady Nyassa*, which Livingstone, irked by the defects of his original Zambezi vessel, the *Ma-Robert*, or *Asthmatic* as he dubbed it, had sent the Expedition's ship's engineer, George Rae (from Livingstone's birthplace of Blantyre), to bring out from Britain in March 1860. All now depended on whether the Rovuma was navigable from its mouth beyond the thirty miles which Livingstone had endured with Bishop Mackenzie the previous March. Livingstone felt that it was worth another attempt. His reviving optimism was echoed by the Expedition's new surgeon-naturalist, Charles J. Meller, who had come out to take the place of John Kirk, whose contract was due to expire. Meller had been with Livingstone in the *Pioneer* in 1861, and, although fever had struck him savagely on the way back from the mouth of the Rovuma, he was able, at the start of 1862, to speak

[1] NLS: Acc. 2365, Livingstone to Dr Tweedie, 2 November 1861.

[2] RGSJ, XXXIII, 1863, p. 264.

'highly of the possibilities of the Ruvuma. Fine high land, strong trees, no bar, healthy land and a bay with 18 fathoms'.[1]

5

DEATHS AND ENTRANCES

After giving up his attempt in Lake Nyasa, at the end of October 1861, to find out about the western extremities of the Rovuma, Livingstone did not return to the direct exploration of the river until eleven months later.

In his final attempt, from 9 September to 8 October 1862, there was a curious combination of the planned and the impulsive. Writers on Livingstone have concentrated on the impulsive. Even Professor Debenham, who has given more serious attention to the Zambesi Expedition and its achievements than any other writer, calls it 'one of his characteristic quick decisions, which were often wise, but were just as often disconcerting to his companions'.[2] To one of them, John Kirk, whom Livingstone persuaded to remain with him in Africa after his contract with the expedition had expired, Livingstone's stubborness in testing again the navigability of the difficult Rovuma seemed to show that he was 'out of his mind': it seemed 'madness'.[3] Yet like so much of Livingstone's apparent lunacy, there was method in his madness.

He had, after all, his instructions from home to explore the river. He also felt that his first two ventures had hardly been given a chance: as he wrote, from the mouth of the Zambezi in July 1862, 'By waiting for the Bishop at Rovuma we failed to ascend very far . . . I am conscious that the delay with the mission rendered our Nyassa trip, as far as concerned the Rovuma question, fruitless.'[4] In spite of these two attempts, he still had inadequate information about the river. (Kirk himself had to admit, in

[1] ZJJS, p. 14.   [2] D, p. 200.   [3] COU, p. 242.
[4] ZEDL, p. 371.

July 1862, that they had 'work to do on the Rovuma'.[1])
By this time, too, Livingstone's anti-slavery reasons for
wishing to circumvent the Portuguese sphere of influence
had acquired new relevance for the Rovuma itself, the
line of which, whether it led directly to Lake Nyasa or
not, was in part one of the routes for the Arab trade from
the centre of Africa to the east coast. Its course would
have to be policed if the slave trade in this area were to be
exterminated. Accurate information, then, was essential
for this purpose.

Since Livingstone's return from Lake Nyasa in November 1861, a chain of disasters had encircled the Expedition. Bishop Mackenzie died tragically at the end of the
year. When his successor came out six months later, it
was clear that the Magomero mission site would have to
be abandoned and probably the whole Universities
Mission to Central Africa transferred from the Lake
Nyasa regions to the east coast. The engines of the
Pioneer proved defective; three months were wasted in
transporting sections of the *Lady Nyassa* to Shupanga
and two months were necessary to assemble them; and
gales drove out to sea again the *Gorgon* which had
brought Mary Livingstone and the representative of the
projected Scottish Free Church Mission, James Stewart,
to the Zambezi in February 1862. Two months later
Mary Livingstone herself was dead. By this time, the
Zambezi and Shire rivers were too low for the *Lady
Nyassa*, when assembled, to navigate them. Supplies
were running short and a trip to Sunley, the British Consul, at Johanna was needed to replenish them. These
varied disasters, together with the personality conflicts
which perennially beset the expedition, cast a sorry light
over it, especially as it had already passed its time limit
with little, apparently, to show for it.

A final journey to the Rovuma might change this im-
pression—and, anyway, Livingstone had intended this all
along. It appears that he made up his mind about the
timing of it, during July 1862, and not in one impetuous

[1] NLS: 2618, folio 279, Kirk to Thornton, 29 July 1862.

moment on 26 August when his provisioning party in the *Pioneer* reached Johanna. As Livingstone wrote to James Stewart from Kongone on 30 July 1862, 'In coming down [the Zambezi] we ran aground three times and saw in the falling water a prospect of a tedious ascent a month or six weeks later. This made us conclude that it may be advisable to spend a few months between August and the rise of the river in November or December in boat exploration of the Rovuma.'[1] The use of 'us' in this passage suggests that unless he was employing it in the fashion of a royal 'we'—which is not unlikely because Livingstone was often over-regal in his communications with the other members of the Expedition—he felt that the decision to explore the Rovuma again at this time was shared with the others on the *Pioneer*.[2]

Clearly, there was a failure of communication. Livingstone had too much on his mind at this time to share his plans in full with the others. He seems to have taken it for granted that they had appreciated all along that he intended to settle with the Rovuma, and that the late summer of 1862 was the most suitable moment for this: hence, the impulsive appearance of many of Livingstone's actions in the last half of 1862. Furthermore, Livingstone, at the best of times a lone wolf, was more than usually unsociable as the *Pioneer* crossed the Indian Ocean to Johanna. He had started to sing to himself in his solitariness. 'If it is *The Happy Land*', noted Kirk, 'then look out for squalls and stand clear. If *Scots wha hae*, then there is some grand vision of discovery before his mind.'[3]

Sir Reginald Coupland, in his pioneering work of Livingstone scholarship, *Kirk on the Zambesi*, felt that Kirk's comments at this time showed that Livingstone was drifting into a 'strange psychological condition'.[4]

[1] ZJJS, p. 209; see also ZEDL, p. 370, Kongone, 25 July 1862, 'We shall go to Johanna and probably Rovuma now.'

[2] Compare COU, p. 239.

[3] Ibid, p. 240.

[4] Ibid, p. 245.

Why? Is there anything strange about the state of mind of a man who has seen many of his plans frustrated during the past five years, and whose wife, having been with him for only two months after a separation of nearly four years, has died suddenly of fever, far away from home and friends? 'It is the first heavy stroke I have suffered and quite taken away my strength,' Livingstone confided to his journal. 'For the first time in my life I feel willing to die.'[1] It was the loss of his wife, undoubtedly, which gave to Livingstone's September 1862 assault on the Rovuma—rash, if not unpremeditated—something of a Nietzschean quality, in the sense that activity, alone, reconciles men to existence. Livingstone wrote to his parents-in-law, the missionary Robert Moffat and his wife, at the end of the venture, 'We have been up the Rovuma about 150 miles and the active life that implies had diminished in some degree the pain which daily visits to the grave kept up.'[2]

Mary Moffat Livingstone had lived in a proper home with her husband for only four out of seventeen years of married life. After their first separation of three and a half years, she had greeted him back to England with some verses, one of which began, 'Do you think I would reproach you with the sorrows that I bore?'[3] In 1862, after her death on the Zambezi, Livingstone was re-proaching himself with them: 'I may be blamed for letting her come and I blame myself very bitterly.'[4] Her death brought out all his ingrained melancholia. Once again, he reflected on his own end: 'I have often wished it might be in some far-off still deep forest.'[5]

In addition to grief at his wife's death and the probings of his conscience, Livingstone carried with him, as he sailed towards the Rovuma in August 1862, unpleasant memories of a painful episode which had taken place shortly after Mary arrived. There had been gossip that she was the not-unwilling recipient of the indiscreet attentions of James Stewart. It was recorded in Kirk's

[1] See B, pp. 298-300.   [2] ZEDL, p. 221.   [3] B, p. 199.
[4] ZEDL, p. 222.   [5] B, p. 206.

journal, although Coupland, when he had access to this document, did not mention the affair. The gossip appears to have been promoted by George Rae, the expedition's engineer, and by Bishop Mackenzie's ageing sister[1] who had gone out with Mrs Livingstone and Stewart to join her brother on the Zambezi. For a while, Kirk had given some heed to the matter. He described Stewart as 'A.1 in the ladies' books', and Mrs Livingstone as 'a queer piece of furniture'.[2] When he came to know Stewart better, however, Kirk realized that it was all 'evil gossip'.[3] So far as David Livingstone was concerned, however, the damage had already been done. One day, before Mary's death, Kirk noted in his journal, 'What must undoubtedly prey upon her mind has been the stories relating to her and Mr Stewart which the latter has unwisely repeated to her and the whole thing has been before her husband.'[4]

Two months later, when Kirk was commenting on Livingstone's singing to himself as they made their way to Johanna, he observed cryptically, 'Probably letters received about his wife's goings on *at home* have vexed him.'[5] There was, no doubt, nothing more immoral in these 'goings on' than in the gossip about Mrs Livingstone and James Stewart on the Zambezi. Mary Livingstone, during the frequent and prolonged absences of her husband, sought what solace she could obtain in the society and attentions of others—and if these sometimes seemed indiscreet, it reflects on Victorian narrowmindedness rather than her own lack of standards. Livingstone's mother-in-law, in a letter of consolation to him on Mary's death, came straight to the point: 'As for the cruel scandal that seems to have hurt you both so much, those who said it did not know you both as a couple. In all *our* intercourse with you, we never had any

[1] KZJ, 3-8 February, 7 April, 15-21 April, 4 May 1862. See also CHA, p. 111.

[2] KZJ, 8 February 1862.

[3] Ibid, 4 May 1862.

[4] Ibid, 26 April 1862.

[5] Ibid, 23 August 1862.

31

doubt as to your being comfortable together.'[1] For David Livingstone, the whole sorry business can only have increased his feelings of sadness and his frustration, as he determined, once again, to go up the Rovuma. When his 1862 expedition to the river was over, he had to some extent assuaged his grief by the application of the Carlylean 'gospel of work'. Yet something of the morbidity which his wife's death had brought upon him still remained. Both elements appear in a letter he sent to Thomas Maclear on his way back to Johanna from the mouth of the Rovuma on 27 October 1862. Livingstone wrote

I suppose that I shall die in the uplands and that somebody else will carry out the plans I have longed to put into practice. I have been thinking a great deal since the departure of my beloved one about the region whither she has gone and imagine, from the manner the Bible describes it, that we have got too much monkery in our ideas. There will be work there as well as here, and possibly not such a vast difference in our being as is expected . . . I work with as much vigour as I can and mean to do till the change comes, but the prospect of a home is all dispelled.[2]

Livingstone could see clearly that his family ties, always tenuous because of long separations, were loosening beyond repair. He had lost his wife; and he had long felt that he was losing, in a spiritual if not in a physical sense, his eldest child, Robert. Robert Livingstone was born in Africa in 1846, a year after Livingstone's marriage, and had gone back to Scotland with his mother in 1852. During the next ten years, he was a constant anxiety to his father, resenting education and parental control. There was much of David Livingstone's own stubbornness and spirit of independence in Robert; but, unlike his father, who had had a settled home life as a boy and was not separated from his parents until he went, as

[1] B, p. 302: Blaikie merely quotes this passage and says nothing of the nature of the 'cruel scandal'.

[2] ZEDL, p. 376.

a young man, to study medicine in Glasgow, these qualities in Robert Livingstone had little chance to mature in
constructive channels. Livingstone seems to have realized
this, on his way out to the Zambezi in 1858, when he
wrote to Robert, 'You are now alone in the world and
must seek His friendship and guidance, for if you do not
lean on Him, you will go astray and find that the way of
transgressors is hard.'[1] Similarly, in another letter to his
son in 1861, Livingstone declared, 'I fear from what I
have observed of your temperament that you will have to
strive against fickleness.'[2] Two years later, his worst fears
for Robert were realized: 'Bad company, and I fear drink,
have been at work on him.'[3]

Robert's 'unsettled state' was a constant worry to his
mother. 'It might have done both good if he had come
out with her,' Livingstone thought, shortly after her
death.[4] That the matter was weighing on his mind—and
was probably one of the elements provoking his bursts of
solitary singing as the *Pioneer* crossed the Indian Ocean
in August 1862—was obvious from a letter which he sent
at the end of the month to his mother in Scotland, 'I
think it may be best for Robert to come out here for a
while,' he wrote to her, 'I thought education the best
legacy I could leave him, but so thought not he and must
rank in life accordingly.'[5] A year later, Robert Livingstone was in South Africa *en route* to seek his father's
advice on his future. But he never reached him; instead,
he made his way to America from South Africa, enlisted
in the United States Army and died of wounds in a Con-
federate prisoner-of-war camp in North Carolina on 5
December 1864 at the age of eighteen.

This legacy of neglect preyed on Livingstone's mind as
he set forth for the Rovuma in August 1862. It was a
neglect which could be justified, perhaps, by the range of
his aspirations and ambitions. But it was something of
which he was deeply, if not despairingly, conscious, a
sacrifice whose purpose he would question when he was

---

[1] B, p. 254.   [2] Ibid, p. 286.   [3] S, p. 452.
[4] Ibid, p. 421.   [5] ZEDL, p. 216.

only four days up the Rovuma on 13 September 1862:
'Am I to experience that this cause is to be founded on
my sacrifice and cemented by my suffering?'

6

THE THIRD ATTEMPT

This expression of Livingstone's personal agony was
scribbled in a little field notebook for 23 August 1862 to
19 March 1863 which covers the period from the start of
his exploration of the Rovuma by boats until his return to
the Zambezi. This, with related accounts and papers,
forms the substance of this book. They provide an
account of the 1862 Rovuma journey which need not be
repeated here. A few preliminary words of comment and
explanation, however, may help in the appreciation of
this document. (More are given on pp. 57-9 below immediately before the field notebook itself.)

As Livingstone and his party set off for the Rovuma in
two small boats (he and his brother Charles in one; John
Kirk and the Blantyre engineer, George Rae, in the other,
although Rae had to return after two days, because of
severe dysentery, the cause, perhaps, of the chronic
stomach ulcer from which he died in 1865), he launched
into a venture that was to bring the mounting criticism of
the Zambezi Expedition to a head and to lead to its
eventual recall. When a letter about this Rovuma journey
which Livingstone wrote to Sir Roderick Murchison,
President of the Royal Society, was published in *The
Times* on 20 January 1863, it provoked a fierce reaction.
It was called

a letter of very instructive yet melancholy character . . . for
it described the approaching fall, if ever there really was a
rise, of the East African Mission. . . . We were promised
cotton, sugar and indigo . . . and, of course, we get none.
We were promised trade; and there is no trade, although
we have a Consul at 500 l. a year. We were promised con-

34

verts to the Gospel, and not one has been made. . . . In a word, the thousands subscribed by the Universities, and the thousands contributed by the Government, have been productive only of the most fatal results. To say nothing of the great mistake of attempting to establish a mission and a colony among remote savages, the first great blunder was to attempt to plant them in the foreign territory of an European nation; for wherever Dr Livingstone attempted to set himself down he found that he was on what had been Portuguese territory almost from the time of Vasco da Gama. The blunder being at length discovered, Dr Livingstone's hopes are now set on the river Rovuma, the boundary of the Portuguese territory. His own description of the Rovuma, and his voyage up it, is truly instructive. The mouth of the Rovuma is about 10 degrees only from the Equator. It took him a whole month to ascend it in canoes for a distance of 156 miles; in other words, his course was at the rate of about five miles a day. Then he was stopped by impassable cataracts and was, by his own reckoning, still three days' journey distant from the Lake Nyassa, the point at which he hopes for trade. The object to which Dr Livingstone points is the establishment of a British trade between this lake and the sea, and the feasibility of this scheme may be estimated by his own account. He says nothing of the harbour at the mouth of the river, which is three quarters of a mile broad, but navigable only for loaded boats drawing eighteen inches, and this only for part of the year. After a month's voyage, even with unladen boats, we are still, by three days of a roadless journey through the jungle, distant from the lake of promise. As to the quality of the country on the Rovuma, Dr Livingstone describes it as of a gray colour, with here and there a green tree, having a few patches of cultivation in a forest. He ascribes this unpromising landscape to the time of his visit being the winter season, although we have never heard before that in the 10th degree of latitude there was any material difference between summer and winter. Then as to the inhabitants of this strange land of hope. 'We passed,' says the learned and reverend gentleman, 'lots of people

35

right civilly, but another lot of these river pirates followed us until there was only a narrow passage under a high bank, and then they let drive their arrows into us. We stopped and expostulated, and for peace' sake gave them 30 yards of calico. All this time we were within 40 yards of a party which had arrived, with muskets and bows, on the high bank. On parting with these we moved on, as we thought on friendly terms, but proceeding we received a volley of musket balls and arrows, but finding that instead of running away we returned the fire, they took to their heels.' Here, as he had done on the River Shire, we find our missionary enacting the part of Mahomet without his success. But we ask, on what grounds does Dr Livingstone pronounce his assailants in this case to have been specially 'river pirates'? For they seem to us to be really nothing else than the ordinary inhabitants of the country, inhospitable, rapacious, and hard of conversion to Christianity. Equally gratuitous seem to be his insinuations of a certain amount of industry among those whom he denounces as pirates. 'They had', says he, 'plenty of grain stowed away in the woods.' How could the learned gentleman ascertain that there was plenty of grain, or any grain at all, in woods which he had not visited, the property of a people with whom his intercourse was hostile? Of the same character is his assertion that the people, of whom he saw little and knew less, 'produce large quantities of oil-yielding seeds'. This large quantity seems to us, even by his own showing to amount to no more than that he may have seen a few patches of sesame, the most easily-cultivated and the poorest in produce of all oil-giving plants. In the same strain is the following:—'Much trade is carried on in canoes bringing rice to exchange for salt, and we never saw ebony of such size as we saw on the banks of the Rovuma.' Who ever before heard of much trade carried on by canoes? and as to the boasted big ebony trees of the Rovuma, we beg to observe that the whole value of the ebony imported into this country does not exceed 20,000 l. and that if the east coast of Africa furnished the whole of it, and it furnishes no part at all, it would not be worth the mission or the consulship. It is a pity that language so unmeasured should be employed on such slender occasions . . . we must come to the conclusion that the time has arrived when the hopeless enterprise undertaken on his advice ought to be relinquished.[1]

This unfavourable comment on Livingstone was reprinted in *The Times* on 20 January 1863. A fortnight later, politely but none the less clearly, the Foreign Secretary, Earl Russell, echoed these sentiments in a despatch to Livingstone recalling the Expedition. He wrote

Whatever may be the natural resources of the newly discovered regions a point on which her Majesty's Government have as yet scanty information, and whatever the extent to which those resources might be developed if frequent and easy intercourse with the interior could be permanently established, it is clear that the route by the Zambesi is one which would be attended with serious if not insuperable difficulties, and her Majesty's Government learn from your last despatches the failure of your attempt to find an independent route by means of the river Rovuma.[2]

Matters had been made worse when Kirk and a coxswain shot, in self-defence, a couple of Africans on the Rovuma—an episode which Livingstone seems nowhere to mention. James Stewart summed up the whole unhappy business tersely in his journal: 'Exploration of the Rovuma turns out a failure. Nothing can be made of that river. Natives bad characters. Livingstone's account still overdrawn.'[3]

The Portuguese were equally critical: not simply because they resented a foreigner's attempts to circumvent their interests but because, with their long experience of the recalcitrant geography of the area, Livingstone's projects had seemed hopeless in advance.

[1] This diatribe was quoted in *The Times* from the *Examiner*: its author is not given.

[2] ZEDL, p. 379.

[3] ZJJS, p. 187.

Governor-General Almeida wrote home to Portugal in
1862,

Good intentions are giving birth to one deceptive scheme
after another out here . . . Dr Livingstone, too, having seen
the Zambezi in flood, has failed to navigate it in the low
periods when it lacks both use and dignity; and driven
from the Shire by its cataracts, has turned to the Rovuma.[1]

To the colonial Portuguese, it has been said, Livingstone 'was simply a peevishly opinionated tenderfoot who
ran into trouble because he would not listen to advice'.[2]

Kirk, in his private journal, was even more scathing:
Livingstone's rashness, he felt, was merely the result of
his desire for 'geographical glory'.[3] 'That Rovuma con-
cern', he wrote to his brother early in 1865, 'was a great
blunder. I think had Rae been against it it might have
been stopped.'[4] When Sir Reginald Coupland published
his *Kirk on the Zambesi* in 1928, he drew heavily on this
journal. He could only conclude that Livingstone's
Rovuma venture of 1862 was 'a miserable and fruitless
month'.[5] Yet, as the episode of the gossip about Mrs
Livingstone and James Stewart shows, Kirk could be
wrong on occasion. His criticism, therefore, of Livingstone on the Rovuma in September 1862, justified though
it often was, ought not to be taken as uniformly valid—
although, included in Coupland's persuasive writing, it is
difficult to resist its force.

[1] Quoted in T. Price, 'Portuguese Relations with David
Livingstone', *Scottish Geographical Magazine* (Edinburgh),
LXXI, 3, 1955, p. 143.

[2] Ibid.

[3] KZJ, 16 and 18 September 1862.

[4] LMB: Kirk letter of 26 January 1863, from River
Shire, Elephant Marsh. It is not clear why Kirk supposed
that Rae might have been able to exercise such influence on
Livingstone, unless he presumed that Rae's experience of
the North Atlantic run might have added authority to his
opinion.

[5] COU, p. 244.

Many recent writers have been less critical of Livingstone. Mr George Seaver, noting Kirk's comments that the water level of the Rovuma was much lower in 1862 than it had been when they were on it in 1861 and was, in 1862, confined to a single channel, observes that it may 'not have occurred to Kirk that the single narrow channel at least indicated where the depth of the water lay, which had been concealed when the shallows were covered'.[1]

In Professor Debenham's study of Livingstone the geographer, in 1955, the significance of Livingstone's stubborn attempts to explore the Rovuma seems finally to be established. Negative results, Professor Debenham points out, can often be as valuable as positive in exploration. Livingstone's 1862 expedition on the Rovuma may have been 'miserable' but it was certainly not 'fruitless'.

It had much to do with the decision of British missionaries and traders that, after all, the Shire was the only practicable approach to Nyasaland . . . the Nyasaland of today is largely the result of that negative but supremely important journey and . . . in his uncouth way Livingstone showed finer qualities of leadership in pressing on against the wishes of all his men than in most of the other subsidiary journeys of this period.[2]

Furthermore, as Livingstone's field notebook for this period indicates, his Rovuma journey of 1862 had a profound psychological importance for him. Livingstone's habit of using these notebooks has been well described by James I. MacNair:

[1] S, p. 416.

[2] D, p. 201. Compare the opinion of the first British Commissioner and Consul-General in Nyasaland, H. H. Johnston: 'Although this latter river [the Rovuma] turned out a great disappointment as far as its navigability was concerned, still its valley was and is a natural highway from the coast to Nyasa, and Livingstone was instinctively right in wishing to open it up.' (Sir Harry Hamilton Johnston, *Livingstone and the Exploration of Central Africa*, London, 1891, p. 264.)

It was his custom to carry in his jacket-pocket a stiff-covered little book in which he made notes, sketches and rough maps. Later, as the opportunity offered, these jottings were elaborated and entered, carefully written in large, strongly-bound volumes of the size of a family Bible. The penmanship of the rough notes is of a very rapid writer, but is generally easy to read.[1]

The field notebook is of the pattern that MacNair describes, with two exceptions. Its jottings, if J.P.R. Wallis's edition of the materials of the Zambezi Expedition is any guide,[2] do not appear to have been written up later to any notable extent in 'large, strongly-bound volumes'; indeed, they were only used very selectively in Livingstone's book about the Zambezi Expedition. And the penmanship is not 'generally easy to read'. The rough notes in the 1862 Rovuma field notebook, interspersed with rapid sketches, are scattered in little order throughout; and, although a general chronological pattern is observable, days and months are sometimes set down out of order, particularly for the period of February and March 1863, when Livingstone was back on the Zambezi. It is also strange that this particular notebook appears to have become separated from the main corpus of Livingstone material in the hands of the family. This is, perhaps, the reason why it was not noted or transcribed in Wallis's edition. It is well known that Livingstone was an inveterate maker of hasty notes on anything that lay at hand; but this little book seems to have a more than usually hectic quality. From all this, would it be unreasonable to say that it reflects the disturbed and distressed condition of Livingstone's mind and spirit at this time?

Certainly, it contains morbid passages which seem to

[1] James I. MacNair, editor, *Livingstone's Travels* (London, 1954), pp. xiii-xiv.

[2] ZEDL: See p. liv, where it appears that this Rovuma field notebook belongs to what Wallis calls the B and C Groups.

reveal his spiritual state as he pushed doggedly up the Rovuma: for example, the forebodings of his own death in the entries for 13 and 25 September 1862; the cryptic note on the methods of embalming bodies used in the American Civil War (8 December 1862); and what appears to be an attempt to sketch out a notice in Portuguese for his wife's gravestone (page 151).[1]

The little notebook also offers evidence about Livingstone's feelings towards his subordinates. There is the burst of rough good humour at Rae's expense at the beginning. But there is the manifestation of Livingstone's frequent frustration with his subordinates in such lines as 'carelessness and selfishness of underlings—an engineer taking the pet or neglecting his work' (26 January 1863): a sentiment which brings to mind Livingstone's belief that it was the incompetence of his engineers that kept Mary Livingstone's vessel stuck for two months in country where she was bound to contract fever.[2] And then, as his Rovuma party were at Johanna on their way

---

[1] The actual inscription in Portuguese on the gravestone is AQUÍ REPOUSÃO / OS RESTOS MORTAES DA / MARIA MOFFAT / A CARA ESPOSA DE / DOUTOR LIVINGSTONE / EM ESPERANÇA / DE RESUREIÇÃO / E FELICIDADE / PELO NOSSO SALVADOR / JESUS CHRISTUS / FALLECIDA / EM SHUPANGA / 27 DIA DE ABRIL 1862 / DA IDADE 41 ANNOS.
The English on the other side reads HERE REPOSE / THE MORTAL REMAINS OF / MARY MOFFAT / THE BELOVED WIFE OF / DOCTOR LIVINGSTONE IN HUMBLE HOPE / OF A JOYFUL / RESURRECTION BY / OUR / SAVIOUR JESUS CHRIST / SHE DIED / SHUPANGA HOUSE / 27 APRIL 1862 / AGED 41 YEARS
(From Filipe Gastão de Almeida de Eça, *Inéditos do Dr. David Livingstone?* (Laurenco Marques, 1953), p. 22. I am grateful to Mr T. Price for correcting a few mistakes in the Portuguese transcription in this book, by checking, personally, the gravestone at Shupanga.

[2] Compare RGSP, VI, 1862, p. 20.

back to the Zambezi, there had been the trouble caused by British sailors striking Africans. Livingstone was terse about this in the entry for 5 November 1862, where he simply describes putting up a notice in the *Pioneer* forbidding such strikings without his permission. The actual notice was more trenchant: 'I regret to be obliged to issue such an order to Englishmen who are not slave drivers but servants of Her Majesty.'[1] With all these problems weighing on his mind, Livingstone could not help complaining on 9 December 1862 that his salary was no greater than 'one of the lowest clerks in the Foreign Office'. Such quips in the Rovuma notebook meander on a curious course with jottings on the death of his wife, strictures on his subordinates, sketches and measurements of many kinds, and purely scientific observations. Altogether, they make it essential evidence for the manifold complications of Livingstone's life at its climax.

7

THE FINAL ATTEMPT

In November 1862, when Livingstone arrived at Quelimane on his return from the Rovuma, a Portuguese observer 'thought that he entered the town like a cat with his tail between his legs'.[2] How much of this apparent despair was due to Livingstone's failure to bring the Rovuma exploration to a successful conclusion and how much to his domestic difficulties cannot be determined. A despondent note was to creep into his journals during the next two years.[3] But, as his first important biographer, Blaikie, pointed out, 'It must not be thought that he had thrown aside the motto which helped him, as much as it had helped his royal countryman, Robert Bruce—*Try*

[1] LMB: *Zambesi Expedition Journal*. This is not used in ZEDL.

[2] cha, p. 174.

[3] Compare B, p. 337.

again.'[1] For once, the snobbish flourish which too often disfigures Blaikie's work makes his meaning clearer. That Livingstone was determined to try again was apparent in a letter that he wrote to James Stewart from Shupanga just before Christmas 1862. 'The Portuguese difficulty', he told Stewart, 'will be got over somehow or other. We have always a loophole by Rovuma, though not equal to Zambesi.'[2]

A month before the instruction recalling the Expedition reached Livingstone, he showed that he still envisaged the possibility of another boat exploration of the Rovuma. This appears from the entry in his journal for 13 June 1863, when he recorded that 'Mr Rae proposes to build a small boat for the small engine at Tette, 45 ft by 8, and 10 inches draught for Ruvuma'.[3] The idea had probably been in Livingstone's mind as he left the Rovuma in October 1862, when he noted that the river would 'require a vessel, drawing 18 inches only when loaded for trade during six or eight months in the year'.[4] Lest such remarks should suggest a totally unrealistic obsession with the Rovuma on Livingstone's part, it should be noted that even Kirk, after the 1862 expedition claimed that,

while the Zambesi remains shut, the Rovuma afforded an easy way by which to pass the hostile and extortionate coast-tribes, and so give a good start for any explorers bound to the unknown regions between the Lakes of the interior, and so determine the yet vexed question where the Nilotic Lakes receive their supplies of water.[5]

This was precisely Livingstone's own view by this time. His Rovuma journey of 1862, in penetrating the mainland to a distance of one hundred and fourteen miles in a straight line (and about a hundred and fifty-six by the course of the river) had shown that Lake Nyasa was within practicable reach by land. The line of the Rovuma, therefore, would be Livingstone's route into the interior on his next expedition.

[1] Ibid. [2] ZJJS, p. 215. [3] ZJDL, p. 238. [4] Ibid, p. 375.
[5] RGSJ, XXXV, 1865, p. 167.

Consideration of the form that this would take filled the eighteen months Livingstone spent in Britain after his return from Africa on 23 July 1864. His friend, Sir Roderick Murchison of the Royal Geographical Society, suggested that he should look into the unsolved problems of the watersheds of southern Africa and indicated the Rovuma as a possible approach. After stressing that he would not consider such a venture as purely geographical but would combine with it his usual anti-slavery and missionary motives, Livingstone told Murchison that he had already made up his mind, on his forthcoming expedition, 'to go up the Rovuma, pass by the head of Lake Nyassa and away west or north-west as might be found practicable'.[1] As soon as his book on the Zambezi Expedition was finished, he would be off.

Livingstone's descriptions of his encounters with the Rovuma in this book are curiously flat and give little indication of the continuing attraction of the river for him. This flatness has often been contrasted with the livelier prose of this first work, the *Missionary Travels*. It may in part have been due to the sharing of the authorship with his brother, Charles, and to the restraint which he was compelled to exercise when he came to episodes in which Charles Livingstone featured, because of his brother's egregious unpopularity with the other members of the Expedition. The absence of an adventurous note in the passages on the Rovuma might be attributed to Livingstone's repeated disillusionment with the river—until one remembers that, throughout the period of composition, he was considering using the river again for his next venture into the interior. It is, however, curious that he does not mention Kirk's killing of one of the Africans who attacked them during the 1862 Rovuma journey. It has been suggested that this may have been because Livingstone, having decided on the Rovuma as his route into central Africa on his next expedition, felt that it would be bad public relations to mention the killing, justified though this may have been.[2] This sug-

[1] B, pp. 349-50.   [2] D, p. 202.

gestion is not entirely acceptable. At least eighteen months before Livingstone returned to England and started work on his book, his report to the Royal Society of his 1862 Rovuma journey, with its account of the 'village where two human heads had been cut off' and the attack on his party by 'the Border ruffians who at various points present obstacles to African exploration', had been published in the press. It is true that, in this report, as in his book, Livingstone did not mention Kirk's killing; but he had shown enough of the disturbed state of the Rovuma to discourage many potential backers of another expedition. This is obvious from the long passage of criticism of the 1862 Rovuma journey which has been quoted on pages 35-7. Further confusion is revealed when one's attention is drawn[1] to the misplacing of what ought to have been one of the exciting passages in Livingstone's book—the account of exploration by boats of the Rovuma. On the way back to the river mouth, a hippopotamous got under their boat, took a bite at it, and was shot in the ear by Kirk. In the book, Livingstone's flat account of this episode is placed almost as if it were in the early stages of their *ascent* up the Rovuma. (See pp. 181-2 below.) In all, perhaps no other explanation of the deficiencies in Livingstone's account is needed, than his weariness: all the unhappy associations of the period, personal and professional, weighing upon his spirit and making him want to hurry through this distressing stage of his narrative as quickly as possible.

Further distress was in store for Livingstone during the eighteen months he spent in Britain before his return to Africa for his last journey. His loneliness was increased by the death of his mother in June 1864 and, at the end of the year, by the news from America that his son, Robert, whom he had hoped to take with him on his new expedition,[2] had died in Lincoln's army. In less than three years, Livingstone had lost wife, mother and eldest son. His last attempt at the Rovuma, therefore, was set in circumstances of increasing personal isolation which

[1] s, p. 419.   [2] D, p. 218.

45

might have broken any ordinary man. But, as Livingstone's great journey of 1852-6 had shown, he often worked best when alone. Three months after he was back in Africa in 1866, and again at the mouth of the Rovuma, he set down in his journal

Now that I am on the point of starting another trip into Africa I feel quite exhilarated. . . . The mere animal pleasure of travelling in a wild unexplored country is very great—the effect of travel on a man whose heart is in the right place is that the mind is made more self-reliant: it becomes more confident of its own resources—there is a greater presence of mind.[1]

Livingstone needed all his presence of mind when he drew into the bay of the Rovuma on 22 March 1866. He had with him thirty-six African and Asian employees, six camels, three buffaloes, a calf, two mules and four donkeys—desperate expedients to meet all the difficult transport problems which he well knew that he would have to face. These expedients created problems of their own. The camels caused all the trouble at first. The dhow which carried them could not penetrate the mangrove swamps at the start of the river. Livingstone found the Rovuma 'quite altered'[2] from what it had been when he first visited it in 1861. At that time, the commander of the *Pioneer* had 'found soundings of three fathoms or more'[3]: in March 1866, the entrance to the river was practically impassable. Livingstone noted in his journal that 'the freshets form banks inside the mouth, which are probably washed out into the deep bay, and this periodical formation probably has prevented the Arabs from using the Rovuma as a port of shipment'.[4] It was a curious obser-

[1] LJ, pp. 13-14.

[2] Ibid, p. 11.

[3] Ibid. D. J. May, the pilot of the *Pioneer*, wrote a brief account of his 1861 experiences in 'The River Rovuma', RGSP, VI, 1862, pp. 36-7.

[4] LJ, p. 11.

46

vation. Why, if Livingstone had been aware that the Arabs had not used the Rovuma as a port, had he been so persistent in his attempts to turn it into one?

In March 1866, at the start of his last journey, Livingstone's approach into the interior required to be made twenty-five miles to the north of the Rovuma, at Mikindani. This had been recommended to him by a British naval officer as the finest port on the east coast. From Mikindani, it took Livingstone's party a week to reach the Rovuma; and they struck the river close to the point where his 1861 expedition had turned back. For three months, Livingstone followed the course of the river. Unpleasant memories of former visits accompanied him. He encountered 'a wall-eyed ill-looking fellow'[1] who had attempted to attack his party in 1861; and he came across the ruins of two villages from which sorties had been made upon his boats in 1862.[2] The suspicions which he had acquired on these two former journeys of the extent of the slave trade on the Rovuma were confirmed. Livingstone's observations of it had then been made from the river; in 1866, on foot, he could see its devastating effects the more clearly. In a sentence which his Victorian editors omitted from his posthumously published journals, he bore blunt witness to the nature of the Rovuma slave trade: 'A child could not go behind the house to make water unless her grandmother stood near her and watched so that she was not stolen.'[3]

Livingstone's last Rovuma journey, however, was not all dangers and disappointments. He appeared in it, at times, in the unaccustomed role of musician. Again his Victorian editors seem to have overlooked the sentence in his journal for 28 April 1866: 'People all listen to my accordion with intense delight.'[4]

[1] Ibid, p. 25.

[2] Ibid, p. 32.

[3] LMB: field note-book, 14 May-30 June 1866; entry for 18 May 1866.

[4] LMB: field note-book, 4 April-10 May, 1866; entry for 28 April 1866.

Livingstone's party pushed on beyond the Nyamatolo Island, the furthest point he had reached in 1862, until they came to the village of the Yao chief, Mtarika, in the first week of July 1866. They then turned south-west to follow an overland route which brought them eventually to Lake Nyasa. After 12 July 1866[1] Livingstone never saw the Rovuma again. In the remaining seven years of his life, until his death at Chitambo's village in what is now Northern Rhodesia, he was obsessed with another river: the Nile and its much sought-after sources. He died hoping these might be found in Central Africa. Livingstone's 1866 journey had destroyed any illusions he might have had about the sources of the Rovuma.[2] It did not, it was clear, rise in Lake Nyasa; nor as the frequent cataracts showed only too clearly, could it become even a partial waterway into the Lake. Yet Livingstone still had faint hopes that something might come eventually of his dream of the Rovuma as a route into the Nyasa interior. As he jotted down wistfully in his journal on 19 May 1866, 'It is strange if all should prove a myth'.[3]

8

AFTERMATH

One myth about the Rovuma which Livingstone created was not dispelled until sixteen years later. On his 1862 expedition he had noticed traces of coal in the sandbanks of the river; and in 1866 he had observed from it 'the dim

[1] LMB: field notebook, 2 July-4 September 1866; entry for 12 July 1866, 'The last Rovuma stream, the Liyombe, was crossed this morning.'

[2] LMB: field notebook, 14 May-30 June, 1866; entries for 19 May 1866 (the Rovuma has 'so many cataracts no canoe could go up into the Lake Nyasa') and 12 June 1866 ('Rovuma rose from fountains among mountains near to Nyassa but not in the Lake itself').

[3] Ibid, entry for 19 May 1866.

outline of distant highlands, in which seams of coal are exposed'.[1] He felt that there might be a coal-field from the Zambezi to the Rovuma 'if not beyond it'.[2] It was the beginning of a dream of commercial possibilities akin to Livingstone's vision of a cornucopia of cotton in Central Africa: the prospect of the industrial Lanarkshire of his adolescence transferred to the heart of Africa.

The attentions of the Sultan of Zanzibar were excited by Livingstone's reports of coal somewhere in his dominions. Sayyid Barghash sent first an Arab and then a Parsee engineer to report on the riches of the Rovuma. Both spoke in glowing terms of its valuable minerals. Fortunately for the Sultan, John Kirk was by this time British Consul at Zanzibar. His experiences of Livingstone's Zambezi Expedition had made him wary of his old leader's claims. Kirk, therefore, suggested to the Sultan of Zanzibar that an experienced geologist should be sent to check on the findings of his Arab and Parsee 'experts'. Who could be better than Joseph Thomson, a young Scot who had taken part in a pioneering geological survey of the east African hinterland in 1879-80, had met the Sultan and possessed the best of qualifications: the medal in geology in Professor Archibald Geikie's advanced class at Kirk's old University of Edinburgh? Thomson was enrolled in the Sultan's service. In 1882 he went down the river and came back to Zanzibar with a negative report: 'the coal-beds of the Rovuma had no existence'.[3] The Sultan was annoyed: it seemed likely, at one time, that his chagrin would prevent Thomson from organizing in Zanzibar a caravan for his expedition into Masailand, on which his fame today largely rests.

Although the Sultan of Zanzibar's dreams had been destroyed, hope for the Rovuma was not abandoned. When Joseph Thomson's account of his journey down

[1] LJ, p. 41.

[2] ZT, pp. 439-40 (see page 191 below).

[3] J. B. Thomson, *Joseph Thomson* (London, 1896), p. 81. See also Joseph Thomson, 'Notes on the Basin of the River Rovuma, East Africa', RGSP, IV, 1882, p. 71.

the river was discussed at a meeting of the Royal Geographical Society in London in 1882, Kirk was present. Although he admitted that the Rovuma looked unpromising, 'Still', says the report of the meeting, 'he thought the riches were there.'[1] The riches this time, suggested Kirk, lay in rubber. Perhaps if this had not become the staple of Leopold II of the Belgians' 'heart of the darkness', the Independent State of the Congo, the experiment of rubber cultivation might have been tried along the banks of the Rovuma. But, by 1882, its economic pipe-dreams were spent; and, when the river became a German possession in 1886, a British highway into Lake Nyasa that did not go through foreign territory was out of the question. Sixty years and two World Wars were to pass, during which the banks of the Rovuma changed hands between the Germans, the Portuguese and the British, before what was to be southern Tanganyika became the scene for a new economic will o' the wisp: the dream in 1947 of visionaries, in Britain and Africa, of a bonanza of groundnuts.[2] The 'large quantities of oil-bearing seeds' which Livingstone had reported in 1862 were, perhaps, an element in the mirage of the hungry men of the 1940s.

To write in such terms is almost to revert to the view that Livingstone's hopes for the Rovuma showed that 'his zeal and imagination much surpassed his judgement'. Professor Debenham's view of the importance of the negative results of Livingstone's exploration of the Rovuma must be recalled in order to redress the balance. Furthermore, in an age of independent East and Central African States, the experiences of David Livingstone with the Rovuma and of those who pursued his hopes until 1882—if not later—may have important lessons to teach: for Livingstone raised, if he did not answer, difficult questions about the communications between Central

[1] RGSP, IV, 1882, p. 87.

[2] *A Plan for the Mechanized Production of Groundnuts in East and Central Africa* (London, 1947: cmd, 7030); Alan Wood, *The Ground Nut Affair* (London, 1950).

Africa and the East African coast and the natural resources of these areas which must be solved before complete economic and political viability can be assured for these states.

In their search, moreover, for an 'African personality' to set against the derogatory assertions of those who look upon their inhabitants as inferior beings, some ideological ammunition may be found in Livingstone's thoughts on the nature of the Africans whom he met on the Rovuma. His 1862 venture was too full of feelings of personal grief and guilt for such of his thoughts at that time to have much value here, although even his hectic little field note-book for that period, in its jottings on African customs and languages, bears witness to his sympathetic interest in their cultures. When, however, he came to write his book on the Zambezi Expedition, he included in the Rovuma section a sharp attack on travellers in Africa who looked down upon its indigenous inhabitants (see page 185). Livingstone did not believe that Europeans should make derogatory generalizations about Africans on the basis of individual instances. He had experienced, in the attacks on his boat exploration of the Rovuma in 1862, such individual instances of African treachery. But he did not consider that these warranted the condemnation of Africans as a whole. There were good and bad individuals everywhere. 'Possibly', he wrote in his journal for his last Rovuma journey of 1866, 'the confounding what is true of individuals and to all individuals has been the great stumbling block to men of intellect.'[1] His expression was confusing but his meaning was clear. 'No one', he deduced democratically from this, 'now believes in the worthlessness of the mass of mankind in comparison with the few who were born to govern.'[2] Or, as he had put it the year before in his book on the Zambezi Expedition, 'In reference to the status of the Africans among the nations of the earth, we have seen

[1] LMB: field notebook, 4 April–10 May 1866; entry for 26 April 1866.

[2] Ibid.

nothing to justify the notion that they are of a different "breed" or "species" from the most civilized. The African is a man with every attribute of human kind.'[1] There is evidence that Livingstone left some traces of these sentiments among the inhabitants of the Rovuma valley. In 1877, Chauncy Maples, a representative of the Universities Mission to Central Africa which had recently founded a village for freed slaves in Masasi in what is now southern Tanganyika, made a journey in the valley of the Rovuma and stayed for a while with the Yao chief, Matola. Then, in Maples's words,

While staying with Matola I was told that there was a man who wanted specially to see his English visitors, because he had known something of a white man in old days, and if we were all like him he would like to make our acquaintance. I desired that he might be presented to us. Forthwith he came, a pompous old man, who spoke in a dignified manner, and who evidently had some information to communicate. Over his right shoulder there hung an old coat, mouldy, partially eaten away, but still to be recognized as of decidedly English make and material. 'Whose was it?' I thought, as he began with much mystery to tell of a white man who ten years ago had travelled with him to Mataka's town [a Yao settlement about a hundred miles south-west of Mtarika's on the Rovuma, where Livingstone had stayed a fortnight in 1866[2]], a white man who treated black men as his brothers, and whose memory would be cherished all along that Rovuma Valley after we were all dead and gone. Then he described him,—a short man with a bushy moustache, and a keen piercing eye, whose words were always gentle, and whose manners were always kind, whom as a leader it was a privilege to follow, and who knew the way to the hearts of all men. This was the description this African savage (as men speak) gave of Dr Livingstone. Then he showed me the coat; it was ragged now, he knew, but he had kept it those ten years in memory of the giver, from whom it had been a legacy when

[1] ZT, p. 596.   [2] LJ, pp. 71-83.

52

they parted at Mataka's. To no one but an Englishman would he part with it, but he let me have it as one of Livingstone's brothers (he said), and it now lies in the museum at Charterhouse School, a precious relic of one whose heart bled for Africa.[1]

Half a century later, Livingstone's coat was sent back from the English Public School to a corner of working-class Scotland when the National Memorial to David Livingstone was opened in 1929 in the old house of the Industrial Revolution in which he had been born in Blantyre, Lanarkshire.[2] It remains there as a symbol of all that was best, and, one hopes, most enduring of David Livingstone's associations with the Rovuma.

[1] Chauncy Maples, 'Masasi and the Rovuma District in East Africa', RGSP, II, 1880, pp. 344-5.
[2] James I. MacNair, *The Story of the Scottish National Memorial to David Livingstone* (Glasgow, n.d.), p. 32.

David Livingstone's Field Notebook

FOR 23 AUGUST, 1862 TO 19 MARCH, 1863,

COVERING THE PERIOD OF HIS EXPLORATION

OF THE ROVUMA IN BOATS

AND HIS RETURN TO THE ZAMBEZI REGIONS,

BY WAY OF THE COMORO ISLANDS,

IN THE 'PIONEER'

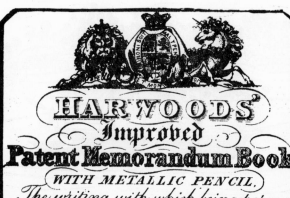

HARWOODS'
Improved
Patent Memorandum Book

WITH METALLIC PENCIL,

The writing with which being perma--nent & the point not liable to break, it is particularly adapted for Merchants, Travellers, Short Hand Writers, &c.

The point to be scraped as required.

In order to protect the Public from numerous imitations of these books, none are genuine unless bearing his signature,

Jno Harwood

Manufactured only by
A. COWAN & SONS,
CANNON ST. WEST, LONDON.

NOTE

This field note-book which is now in the National Library of Scotland, Edinburgh, measures $5\frac{1}{2} \times 3\frac{1}{2}$ inches.

It is bound in black leather, has a pencil-loop on one side, and locks with a small clasp. Manufactured in London, its proprietary mark is *Harwoods' Improved Patent Memorandum Book with metallic pencil.* Livingstone made a practice of using this type of notebook on his explorations in Africa; other brands which he employed were *T. J. and J. Smith's Metallic Book* and *Henry Penny's Metallic Memorandum Books.*[1]

On the cover is a small notice which bears the words (not in Livingstone's handwriting) 'Journey to Rovuma in "Pioneer", 1862'. Although half of the seventy-three leaves deals with Livingstone's return to the Zambezi after his abortive attempt to explore the Rovuma in boats, the anonymous author of this title has clearly seized on the field notebook's main interest. Nevertheless, the second half of it is of value to students of Livingstone because it adds numerous details to the over-succinct account in the *Narrative of an Expedition to the Zambesi and its Tributaries* (London, 1865)[2] of the *Pioneer*'s return to the Zambezi and Shire Highlands during the period from 17 October 1862 to 19 March 1863.

All the sketches and the whole of Livingstone's writing in this notebook appear below. A sloping line (/) indicates the end of a page in the original field notebook. A small row of dots (. . .) indicates an indecipherable word or phrase. Where a transcription is doubtful, it is followed by a question mark in brackets: (?).

---

[1] ZEDL, p. liv.
[2] Compare ZT, pp. 445-55 (below, pp. 195-204).

Livingstone disliked conventional full-stops in his journals and letters and frequently used instead a small dash or a double dash (=). These have been reproduced. No punctuation has been added. It is realized that this often makes for difficult reading. But the addition of punctuation would destroy the staccato character of Livingstone's observations and musings as he went up and then away from the Rovuma in 1862. Furthermore, the insertion of punctuation would unnecessarily clarify Livingstone's thought at a time when he was obviously often uncertain of the drift of his hastily-made reflections and notes. The original spelling has also been preserved.

The field notebook begins with a cover and first page of jottings, largely of a linguistic nature. Although the reproduction of these delays the introduction of the narrative sections of the notebook, it brings out the occasional nature of this and prepares the reader for the frequent disturbance of the narrative sections by Livingstone's administrative, linguistic, scientific and personal jottings.

Some day, one hopes, all of Livingstone's field notebooks (those in the Archives, Salisbury, Southern Rhodesia; in the Memorial at Blantyre, Lanarkshire; and in other libraries and in private hands) will be intensively edited. In this way, much new light will be thrown on the many complicated problems of Livingstone's personality and influence because his field notebooks represent the raw material of his thought and emotion which is only partially revealed in his more substantial journals, his letters and his printed works. But, in the present instance, no elaborate scholarly apparatus is provided, although a few notes have been added for simple explanation and commentary. The general reader should be able to follow the drift of this field notebook with the aid of the introductory essay, the accompanying documents and the extract from the *Zambesi and its Tributaries*. It is hoped that the scholar will want to consult the original field notebook itself: indeed, its many cryptic passages and words will only be finally resolved after many specialists have plumbed its depths.

58

At the start of his African journal for 1854, Livingstone wrote, 'I mean to note down even trivial incidents such as will interest none but myself.'[1] When this 1854 journal was edited for publication in 1963, it was revealed how mistaken Livingstone was. A great man's greatness is often revealed—and his limitations appropriately displayed—as much in his *trivia* as in his *chefs d'œuvre*. It is hoped, therefore, that the 'trivial incidents' of Livingstone's 1862 Rovuma field notebook, in spite of their hectic, often inconsequential form, will prove to have more than a private interest.

Notes marked 'A' or 'B' are printed at the end of the transcript of the notebook. (p. 156)

[1] *Livingstone's African Journal*, 1853-1856, edited by I. Schapera (London, 1963), p. xxiii.

```
30   4  26        40        30
         4         4         4
       ─────     ─────     ─────
   30) 104       112       126
```

mziwa = month

deep —

Nyamchacha

shallow

Kwene = maka

& Kakanue very

Batsamire = ordinary (?)

depth

makwire gentle

yaloa mponda

swallow pole

sink — alobseka

D⁰ — Taika lose/

Juma bin Saidi

Amar bin Salemu

Manabay — where slaves are taken

to in Madagascar

Vungonya rice plant (?)

Mariwe country

Biscuits = Boots

Sugar —   copper

Pork —   spar

Preserved meats

Preserved Potatoes —

Suet   PITCH
Flour
Oil
Candles box
Beef
soap — coffee /

23 Aug 1862

reached Mohilla and waited till 26 then went over to
Johanna. Left ship coaling and went over hills to Pomony
with Kirk & Rae = Road very rough from roots of trees
Many beautiful ferns — Mr. Sunley sent two donkeys to
mount us three miles from his plantation — Rae tried one but
leaped over it then it set off at full gallop with him before he
got hold of bridle — He leaped off & gave a laugh to us that
did us good though I almost fell off the donkey with it.
Recrossed hills and took the King — Sidi drayman[1] & the
Cadi over to Pomony by steam boat — scraped the edge of
coral reef in / going in — Sunley is overhauled by the Govt
for employing slave labour[A] — The Orestes came in on 3rd
and the Captain an excellent man did everything he could
for us and volunteered to tow us over to Rovuma We found

[1] In Gardner's account (below, p. 169) this appears
clearly as *drayman*, in Livingstone's field notebook it might
possibly be read as *dragman*: that is *dragoman*, an interpreter.

[A] See p. 156.

East Pueblo

Vega

B Borealis

α coronal Borealis

coronal Vega

Vega

Arcturus

comet

Mr Received Colliers Newels

sea rough & the Orestes walked away with us with great ease
straining us however much — Hawsers parted on Sunday
morning with the strain — and the Captain asked me if he
would tow me or let me go on alone — I went on alone and in
a few hours saw the Rovuma — He resolved to come up with
us 2 days / £5943 13 3 price of Lady Nyassa[1] [deleted by
Livingstone.]

Left Kongone 6 August 1862 at 3-30 P.M. steam E.

> 35° . 56′ from Vega
> 35 40 from *a* Bootis
> 25° 45′ from α coronal Borealis

8th

Received Collier & Newell[2]

9th Sept 1862

Left Pioneer at anchor in Rovuma bay in charge of Mr
Young[3] and favoured with the company of Captain Gardner
of HMS Orestes with his galley and cutter we ascended
Rovuma & found it very low — spent first night about 12
miles up

[1] It should be remembered that Livingstone paid for the
Lady Nyassa out of his own pocket.
[2] Two members of the *Pioneer's* crew: Charles Collyer
(Second Mate) and 'Newell, A.B.' (from L M B: crew list in
Zambesi Expedition Journal).   [3] Lieut. E. D. Young, R.N.

10th

immense sand banks with winding shallow streams that go
from side to side / saw Lake Chidia from hill on right of
river as we ascend. (left bank name of tsetse ascertained to be
chipanga =

11th Sept 1862

parted with Captain Gardner at Chidia he returning to
Orestes Mr Rae ill with dysentery returned with the captain
People very suspicious and afraid to let articles out of their
hands — we took one man to shew us the way to Lake Chidia
he said 'You will lie and not give me anything' — people
make fine mats and poor houses — ebony near Lake = spend
night on a sand bank of large extent / about two miles below
where steamer turned

12th Sept

off at 6 AM. & came to villages — people not afraid but
difficult language to understand — Breakfast below a knob on
hills on our right. game seems abundant = the water seems to
increase as we ascend — Dr K.[1] has shivers & C.L.[2] had a
touch
C.L. wandered in bush
sleep on sand bank

[1] Dr John Kirk.   [2] Charles Livingstone.

Anchorage	10	28	30
Lat. by Vega	10°	48′	20″

19	50

13 Sept

= off at 6-20 — crossing from side to side came at 1 PM to a part where river is divided into three = we dragged / her over 12 inches of water & she requires at present 18 — we then went into a wrong channel & prepared to spend the night — a man Goñgonda came to speak to us & said the south or Makoa[1] side were at war with them = the edge of a table land apparently rises now to 400 feet & is all covered over with forest — looks as if sandstone — ebony exposed to weather — goes as if burned with charcoal — Prospects look gloomy for a colony by this river / but I will not despair if this road fails another will open — It is a great cause and it has been by the Divine favour & influence that I have been allowed to call it mine — Am I to be a martyr to my own cause — I begin to think that I may not live to see success — Am I to experience that this cause is to be founded on my sacrifice & cemented by my suffering. Every covenant was ratified with sacrifice. I hope this may be consecrated if I die by my death — / since the death of my Mary I often feel that I have not long to live but I will do my duty for all that.

[1] The Makua, a tribe of the area.

... will not despair
if this ... fails and the
will open — It is a great
cause and it has been
by the Divine favour &
influence that I have
been allowed to call it
mine — Am I to be a
martyr to my own
cause — I begin to think
that I may not live to
see success — Am I to
experience that this
cause is to be founded
on my sacrifice &
cemented by my suffering
Every covenant was
ratified with sacrifice
I hope this may be

14 Sept 1862

—the old man Goñgunda brought several others after dark
with fowls cassava and meal—for sale. This morning he
came again & says that the river is deep in front and five
months are required to reach the end where waterfalls are. The
language is very difficult to understand even for Senna[1]
people = yams in plenty = consonants are omitted — ma la ke
instead of zina lache[2] — his name
no alligators here but above & below this they abound = we
spend the / Sunday in the country called *Ndonde*—North
bank—south is called Mabiha where people puncture upper
lips—Ngomano—source of river = slave traders pass up the
river some along bank & some in small canoes but they never
saw boats before—to reach Ngomano where water comes
out the soil 2 mouths
Louma is used instead of Rovuma—went up to Mtaba[3] land
& found all very thickly wooded but brushwood and bamboo
prevail most—a good deal of land cleared & manioc
sorghum = cultivated also some gerzilin & sesamum / women
all ran away but one man stood & having told him we were
only looking at the country he asked if I would drink &
brought a cupful = told him we did not buy people—Rocks
sandstone conglomerate—with rounded quartz pebbles in it

[1] The aSena, another tribe.

[2] Dzina lace: *his name* in the Nyanja language, elements of
which Livingstone had acquired in the Lake Nyasa area.

[3] This might also be interpreted *Mtaka.*

to tatou but teeth pointed

15 Sept. 1862 we return

many new trees — another man says we are ten days from
Ndonde where navigation ceases by hills and cataracts —
there the Quiloa road crosses the Lohuma or Louma
no tatoo but teeth pointed

15 Sept 1862

we returned $\frac{1}{2}$ a mile & got into the / proper channel but it is
still shoal — not enough for the boats — passed a village on
the N bank people stood even the women did not run away
— At night some people came & standing on a sand bank
asked what we wanted — no people appear on the south at all
— man passed us in his canoe & his child set up a loud wail
when turning towards him — took obs[ns1].

16th Sept 1862

many canoes lie on the banks & the river seems as if it had
fallen very recently / came at midday to a village on a sandy
island & soon began a trade in fowls — The men ran after us
till we stopped at 5 P.M and all seem friendly — one man had
a lip ring the first we have seen — he laughed when joked
with about it and said it was his conceit.

17th

came to another tribe on a sand bank
told us to stop but yielding in a small thing leads to more

[1] Observations: sextant readings.

hill on north branch the
3 miles from end of range

hill where we slept
night on 1st & Sept — 1842

demands — Nguzhakara[1] chief came with a horse pistol in a
bag & red cap on — tattoed in dots & teeth / pointed — one
man again with a lip ring   〰〰   〰〰
Njare country & people they live on the sand banks because
the Makua come from the south by night and steal them —
when the river fills they return to the shore — arrived at
5 P.M. at many villages built on sand banks
people say that they flee from Dionde who captures many of
them — Found a bit of *coal*

18th

came to a very bad crossing drew boats up a little way with
help of natives & then turned Dr K. said it would be better
to turn as we might get stuck / on a sand bank and the natives
refuse to help us — I replied that if we risked nothing we
should gain nothing it was but 2 boats we should lose — he
rejoined it was risking more than the river was worth. We
then went back to the proper channel & with one drag got
through. River seems to be falling daily
A detached hill like an igneous one rises in front & the table
land abruptly cut off towards river clears (?) away
Gum copal offered for sale by name sandarwzi
we sleep opposite a / hill on north bank this 3 miles from end
of range
Hill where we spent night of 18th sept 1862
found another bit of coal on the sand — Lat 11° 01′ 19″

[1] Livingstone wrote 'Monekara' then crossed out 'Mone'
and wrote 'Nguzha-' above it.

Long. 39° 20′ 30″ — Dr Kirk affected with sore eyes
a pink ring round cornea & vessels of conjunctiva injected
had pain in temples last night & pulse rises quickly up to 100
& then falls again
tongue furred — to take rousers[1] & put gauze before the eyes
= tobacco cheap = six blocks / a fathom of calico
Hills said to resemble exactly the oolite hills of the
Dardanelles — The valley opens in front or about 39° 17′
East to a large plain where igneous looking hills appear[2]
Maranga a headman of robbers who received cloth

a number of people (19) followed us the morning after first
calling us to go into a short creek
waited for us while we took breakfast then went along the
bank / fully armed till we came to a high bank and a narrow
passage below it — a puff adder lying on the bank was shot
and this they pretended was fired at them — they then went
forward to another high bank & narrow passage under it and
began the war antics — one old man fired an arrow over the
black boat — it lighted two or three yards beyond it & several
more fell short. We stopped and expostulated with them
and allowed three to come behind us brandishing their bows
& arrows / after $\frac{1}{2}$ an hours expostulation & explaining our

[1] Livingstone's jocular manner of referring to his anti-fever pill, a mixture of quinine with a purgative: See Michael Gelfand, *Livingstone the Doctor* (Oxford, 1957), pp. 297-8.
[2] A very small drawing of these hills has not been reproduced because of technical difficulty.

objects & what the shot had been fired at we prevailed on
some to come to the boat. One old man said he had been
robbed by Arabs in boats & he supposed we were the
parties — that no white man could pass up that river & we
must go back or pay cloth — preferring the disgrace of paying
to shedding blood, and putting it on the plea of making
friends I gave two large pieces of cloth about 30 yards
told them we were English & feared to shed blood / because
God saw us: and we did not fight but would defend
ourselves if attacked — shewed how easily we could beat
them off, but for the fear of God — they then began to
quarrel among themselves about the cloth — most increasing
the demand, and it looked as if even a regular plunder of all
we had would not please them — The more we yielded the
more was demanded as they held us in contempt — There /
was no chief among them they being a lot of river pirates
who are constantly plundering & slave hunting — we could
not go back either, as the river is so low we would be
exposed to their arrows at every high bank & narrow
passage & our retreat would be considered victory. The
headman Maranga took cloth & went on promising to give
us food as a token of friendship — when we had as we thought
settled with them another party still on the high / bank
commenced shooting at us with arrows and guns as we
moved on. Four ~~three~~ shotholes were made in our sail —
the arrows missed: though we were not more than 60 or 70
yards off — We then returned the fire and off all ran at once —
I am glad that we tried all we could to pass peaceably & as

73

...grous looking hills in
... - and nearer now
opposite the end of the
... land on the North -
of K. somewhat better
met people coming down
river in canoes: with
all their pots pans &c
as if flitting - one civilly
pointed out the deepest
water without being
asked - They set fire to
reeds on a small island &
drive out the Sensi
passed first rocks in
river as a dyke of
trap as it appeared -
though tufa appeared
in banks some days
since = spend night &
sunday opposite some
...

we told them the guilt was theirs in the last wanton attack =
Slept in boats in the river & kept watch two hours each = A
man observed standing with bow bent yesterday as if to kill
one of us /

20th Sept 1862

more igneous looking hills in front — and we are now
opposite the end of the table land on the North — Dr K.
somewhat better met people coming down river in canoes
with all their pots pans &c as if flitting — one civilly
pointed out the deepest water without being asked — they set
fire to reeds on a small island to drive out the Sensi / Passed
first rocks in river as a dyke(?) of trap as it appeared — though
tufa appeared in banks some days since = spend night &
Sunday opposite some rough igneous looking / rocks & hills
at end of southern table land River rather better since we
saw rocks in it, probably they prevent its flowing away
Tsetse again —
Matingula chief of Makuas at end of hills — chonga = michi
= Néwara range Mokura mountain in front — large —

21st

many people around us — women clothed in bark
chief & people friendly — asked for medicine for ulcers —
many of which are seen — as also Elephantiasis
bought fowls = Reported that Rovuma or Lohuma turns off
to the Northwest & is small / while Niende is the main

fishing ... the
... ... is put
down on the fish &
the ... ...
no hole to catch
... after they are ...

stream & rises in the mountains East of Lake Nyassa known here as *Chirwa* = the point Ngomano is the junction of Lohuma & Niende — Lohuma is narrow — rocky & turbulent — arising where people make salt — fishing basket the broad part is put down on the fish & the hand put in by the hole to catch them after they are in the extinguisher — It is made of wicker work
saw fish are up here /

Caption & words on drawings overleaf
W. end of table land on South bank of Lovuma 21st Sept & 1st Oct 1862
mabiha tribes Marambuaje lands
Nsimbua country
Bank opposite chonga michi
W. end of range on N of Rovuma = Néwara
Nkobe tribes chonga michi
land of Matingula
— Mude — Namomkeri chonga michi

77

أدسو حكم

Livingstone Hakim

بركال د او سى

Birkâl bin ya Obo

21st Sept 1862 Lat 11°.07′ 29″ Long 39° 8′ E
sent a note to Major Pelly[1] by the arab Barkal bin Yaobo
Soomali and as he came this morning to greet gave him one
Pound of powder
he seemed to give the best advice in his power and
particularly warned us against the Makonde — see a man this
morning with a lip ring /

1 michi	Makua
2 mbiri	stations from
3 Bangara	Michi up
4 Ngomano	on N bank
5 = 10 days	up Rovuma

without people but plenty of game — cant pass Nyundo on
account of cataracts

1 Matawatawa	(?)	to Ngomano
2 Malumba = route		
3 Metumbo		some stations
4 Singezi		by Makonde
5 Nyundo		on S. bank

It is said the Makonde have plenty of ivory and are on right
bank of the river — we came to / spend night of 22nd among
them without knowing it — seem civil but we shall see /

Livingstone Hakim

Birkal bin ya Obo soomali — an Arab whom we met at
Michi —

[1] Lewis Pelly, agent of the Government of Bombay at
Zanzibar.

we were amon[g]
Makongio[?]
came I told me a[t]
Rocks in River
heads
Kindula
now
shure

seen from West A

Lat, 11° 09' 19" South
Long. 38 52 E.

Sekumbi Rock
sept 1872

bivouac of
on 23

23 Sept 1862

Cold at nights & strong winds which begin in the afternoon
— we sleep in Matawatawa near a peculiar granite looking
rock — on right bank from South East We were among
Makonde who came & sold meal for beads *written on drawing*
Rocks in River noro kindula shure seen from East
flood rises about 8 feet
ordinary high water as marked on rocks about 3 feet above
the present
Honey offered several times for sale — seems abundant —
artificial / hives are used — stop to speak to an old man who
called out as we sailed past "Father where are you going &
why do you pass without speaking as if it were war" — we
stopped above him and told what we were — asked if he had
seen English before he replied "no but he had heard of
them" — He had seen Banians[1] — Asked why all were living
on sand banks he replied on account of war. with — opposite
Lokumbi hill to sleep — Moedi in front Makonde tribe still /
Lat 11° 09′ 19″ South
Long 38 52′ E

Caption on drawing
bivouac of Lokumbi Rock
on 23rd sept 1862 =

[1] Indian traders from Zanzibar.

Mabonde Tatoo-stomach
TEETh pointed

Tatoo on breast

many
people the
on banks,
see us. pass
us the sérés
but more frequently

Caption on drawing

Makonde tatoo — stomach teeth pointed / Tatoo on breast

24th Sept

people came by night with articles for sale — among other
things sesame or gerzelin, an oil producing seed of
increasing export value =
[*tiny drawing here, with caption*: 'Lokumbi seen from W.']
Rocks again in river above Lokumbi DO DO
at Bangala where river is narrowed between low hills —
Reached after a good deal of hauling a / part of river
enclosed in tree covered hills — and about 200 yards
wide = The country generally has a light grey appearance —
trees numerous but not large except the Baobab and figs =
Here people have hid their corn & grain in bark safes about
$4\frac{1}{2}$ high by $2\frac{1}{2}$ or three feet wide — all plastered with clay —
this may account for few large trees being seen many people
stood on banks to see us pass with sails
but more frequently it was a drag at times (all hands?) / in
the water — we spend the night just below a tree covered
island the first of the kind we have met

25th Sept 1862

come to two tree covered islands with euphorbias and many
climbing plants
Beehives placed on the trees every 100 yards or so

85

An indefinable foreboding of death — was this what pressed
on dear Mary's mind? when she came to the Zambesi —
seven canoes each with two men passed us up river they
were full of stuff / River sown with rocks 2 dykes stretch
across but openings are found — we struck several times
before we stopped at our station of 25th Sept 1862 being
spent at Ngomano

Caption on drawing

Nyamitolo or Nyamitulo island & cataract Lat 11° 13′ 30″
Long 38° 28′ 2(?) turning point of 26th Sept 1862 400 feet
about Bar 29 59

26th Sept 1862

we struck sunken rocks several times yesterday and this
morning found further progress impossible without
dragging the boats over a cataract called from the island
Nyamitolo

It is a mass of low rocks with no great fall for the native
canoes go up and down with ease

we might go up too but the boats would sustain damage in
coming down and before we reach Ngomano three days
distant there are much worse inasmuch as the rocks are
larger and the passages narrower

The distance from this to the mouth of the Loyendi is about
30 miles / but the water just now is only about 15 inches —
If Ndonde at Ngomano had been the man who delivered up
the murderers of Dr Roscher[1] I would have gone to give him
a present = but I dont see what good could be effected by a
three days tramp — The reporters maintain that the water of
the Rovuma come out of Nyassa but in a small stream and
down mountains = people use a spear & line made on same
plan as that for the hippopotamus for killing the alligator
and there are but few of the reptile / People keep their
provisions in field and seem to care much more for
themselves than for the food — They have large provision

[1] Dr Albrecht Roscher of Hamburg who had been sent
out in 1858 from Bavaria to explore Central Africa. Two
months after Livingstone's sighting of Lake Nyasa, he was
in these regions and was killed by some of the inhabitants
of a village near the Lake.

89

Lat. 11° 13' 30 S
Long. 38° 28' Ras

an ant eater along
N. side the guinea
fig house along
double rose of brown
clams was shot
to day — also a
gazelle —

grounds but all live on sand banks where they can fight or
run away when slave traders come — All seem familiar with
canoes women even manage them dexterously — a great
alluvial plain in front and river spread in a rocky bed — no
mountains appear except one conical hill. Tsetse and
antelopes of small kinds abound — cotton of Psreozdran (?)
kind has been cultivated /
Lat 11° 13′ 30 S
Long. 38° 28′ East
an anteater about the size of a guinea pig having a long
flexible nose and of brown colour was shot today — also a
gazelle — Totive by name /
[*The following two pages are occupied by a coloured wash
drawing reproduced on page* 100 *below.*]

27 Sept 1862

came down river past Bangala islet = Mikhōta is sugar cane
but here distinguished by the name foreign
It is evidently from being termed Mikhōta manga an
imported cane and not that in the interior of the country —
They have none here but know it. Gundūe a fish striped
across the body which makes a large round nest in the sand
— taking the material outwith its mouth and spitting it over
the side = It is said to sleep in a hole in the bottom & hide
there during the rains = guards it / chipupa
spend Sunday opposite an island with people
women very naked
men friendly = a large monkey which seemed inclined to

91

woman ... wrapping
... for sale
the ... but: ...
cloth is ... folded
pressed ... through is
as to ... give the
appearance ... of a tail
... many
... rose
to the ... idea of

... their snuff boxes
the lid enclosing
the under part
closing over

shew fight was shot — alligators are caught by a spring trap
and seem to be cowed here — one seldom puts up his nose =
The rock is of a granitic nature probably gneiss but is often
as if stratified & looks like hardened sandstone we turned
when we had gone 169 miles up the river,[1] that is, by adding
Lat & Long together — we have / gone over twice the ground
— Lovuma[2] woman bringing rice for sale the bit of cloth is
folded & passed through so as to give the appearance of a
tail behind and may have given rise to the idea of tailed
tribes in Africa Ri Liènde is reported to branch off from the
Rovuma and run parallel with the Lake
is very large but at this time very / shallow — It is near
Ngomano which seems to be about 30' above where we
turned or say in 38° 00 E & probably in 11° 20″ S

29th Sept 1862

Came down to our worst dragging place & the people
crowding to the boats with fowls & eggs for sale we
remained to breakfast — bought some of their snuff boxes the
lid enclosing the under part or closing over it
passed hill Lokumbi and above sleeping place walked some/
distance inland — There is plenty of ebony but small & the
people clear it off easily by applying fire to the root = Many
large snail shells shew that the land at certain seasons is very

[1] Livingstone was mistaken here: it should be 156. He got
the figure right in the entry for 2 October.
[2] Lovuma = Rovuma on the principle of the
interchangability of the *l* and *r* in Bantu languages.

moist — Offered at last place to buy a lip ring here called
Dōna but the idea seemed to excite the risible faculties of
the ladies very greatly — It must have a meaning *besides
ornament*[1] /

30 Sept 1862

Two of the sailors from the men of war have fever slightly —
people refuse to eat anything offered to them — but took a
few needles scarcely believing they were presents nor
knowing to thank for them
The practice of feeding strangers quite unknown. Much
native trade on river
They go down to buy salt with rice — many on tramp too —
women travelling along shore — men in canoes / had a great
deal of dragging in consequence of mistaking the channel
we went up by — very windy every night

1st October 1862

Morimbue = name of Jalevue (?) our men shot this morning
caffeine is said to be a perfect remedy for poisoning by
opium — Reached Michi before Midday Sobi chief of
Makonde lives on chisure hill in front of chimbara bara,
where we turned Nsimbira to the S W of Marambuanje S. /
Mabiha general name of people on south *Nkobe* on North —

---

[1] If *Dona* in this context is the same as the Portuguese for
Madam, the *meaning* was probably that the lip-ring was a kind
of status symbol.

the bows
are very
simple

Neither men women ... do they find ... well send
the bark ... negroes
... different ... from
... in ... the cloth ...
sometime ... front
... never ... they
... visitors

The arab whom we met here went off with four chains of
slaves
This says Motingula is the general slave route from all the
Lake region & beyond
He says that the Makonde below said that they did not know
we were English and he says he told them that we do no
harm if not molested but if attacked we can bite — offered a
rug but he preferred / cheaper cloth of cotton The chief
Sobi of the Makonde lives in front of where we turned on a
difficult hill called *chisùre* The trade on river is in salt which
is made here $=$ The river has fallen about $2\frac{1}{2}$ inches in ten
days & weather is becoming very hot — Fever cases better $=$
guns are abundant
the bows are very simple affairs compared with those of the
Manganja. The arrows without poison & so shaped /
Neither in men or women do we find the back (?) said to
mark negroes nor is the calf of the leg different from that in
Europeans
sometimes the end of the cloth is spread thin in front but
never do they shew any symptom of being indecent — there
is no steatopyga and the nates are rounded exactly as in
Europeans — They are profusely ornamented with tatoo as
if intended to be seen — colour seems a sort of covering to
them as they dont . . . as naked . . .[1] /

[1] This portion of about five words is indecipherable.

noku e funa
nguo = chuma
fowl wishes
a cloth

Matingula professed to have sent off for rice so that we
might not be in want while in our way down to the sea — The
men have detained us only to / send word on to the Makonde
to be ready for us — He brought a little rice — says that he
heard nothing of any white man having gone to the Lake —
that we are the first. Roscher may have been so mixed up
with the Arab traders that the country people did not know
him

By one way the Rovuma is crossed several times before
reaching the Lake — from Mozambique the Liende must be
crossed — the Mabiha have all the lip ring both men &
women /

2nd October 1862

Alligators eggs were sold to the men last night and this
morning they found a nest with 33 eggs in it. They are
buried in the sand about a foot — They are hatched three
months and are liberated by the rising waters
one set of eggs only per annum
a species of wild coffee abounds and often is laden with
fruit about the size of peas but the branches bend down
It is eaten by the natives —
A new or travelling rate for the chronometer shewing it to
have been − 5s. 2 instead of − 8s. will make our distance /

99

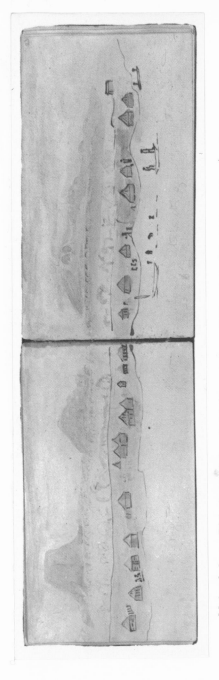

Makonde huts = Right bank of river just below cataracts of Nyamitolo island./ Lat. 11° 13′ 30″ Long. 38° 26′ E. Women pounding corn. Fishermen. 26th Sept. 1862.

about 15′ less on 156 miles. Many wild animals had been at our breakfast place before we stopped at it — Feel depressed when I look at our prospects

There is no hamlet but a mission might be made self-supporting on the Lake but we have the Portuguese eager to gain by the labour & enterprise of others = No general Government wishes to develope trade and of course revenue but the Governors by slavehunting put an extinguisher on lawful commerce and it is / difficult to get men to act honourably even from interested motives

We were bamboozled by one whose interest would have been promoted by serving us honestly—hindered by another who has knocked one of H.M. ships useless on the bar of Lagos & we barely escaped the same fate with Ma Robert to the imposition of which on us he mainly contributed — It would have done him more good in a worldy point of view had he honestly done his duty — Another turned out a thief / Men burning out the reeds in order to secure the senze and other small game but none spoke to us — other English will now be safe — and no demand will be made

4th Oct 1862

Variation of compass at Michi 11° 30′ = W = We came down past a village on a sand bank which had two human heads & where they misled us in going up and they now followed us with a large old goat for sale — We did not stop — came to another village

this village is deserted
because of the death of a
woman: her grave is in
the middle of the huts.
Here there is cotton cultivated
and Brinjal a solanum plant

We had the first shower
of the season this afternoon
only a slight + passing thunder
shower

cotton
meeting hut

the woman's grave on
the hillside where

of more civil people and bought food then to a deserted
village near where we spent our / first journey out (14 Sept)
and remain over tomorrow
This village is deserted because of the death of a woman,
her grave is in the middle of the huts — Here there is cotton
cultivated and Bingals a solanaegous plant
We had the first shower of the season this afternoon only a
short & passing thunder shower
Caption under drawings
cotton
meeting hut
the woman's grave in the village where we /[1]
River Rovuma

6 Oct 1862

we came down past where we spent our first Sunday on the
river = got a large goose = no natives appear after we past a
village in the morning
This part made us at first look on this as a country "to let" —
at midday I went ashore and saw many large Molonipe trees
— also Mosokoso good wood for shipbuilding — one 12 feet
in circumference
ginger growing too & many trees I did not know — a little
marsh lay near /

7th October 1862

cold fogs in the mornings — there is often almost a mile of
  [1] A page is missing here.

season = a thick musty
a mere return
an umbrella with
palm leaf —
there is plenty of
in the country

rich level alluvial land between the bank of the river and the hills It is sparsely covered with trees = bushes = & young palms = goose shot

The natives who accompany us are readily put into a panic or they are noted for thoughtlessness — This morning the second shower of the season = a thick misty one

a man extemporized an umbrella with a palm leaf — there is plenty of game in the country but / it is not seen near the river.

We passed an affluent which discoloured the water below it — unless we could have gone into the country we could not form a correct opinion as to its capabilities — either as to its woods or amount of cultivation but generally the people seemed to have plenty to sell and especially gerzelin or susemme = wild oil seeds of the stericula abound /

8th October 1862

On to the Northern border of the opening in which lies Lake Chidia — went in and found the largest ebony we have seen about 50 yards from the bank — one was about 2 feet in diameter & 20 feet high

several were of this height & nearly as thick as a man's body Madandi fish in great numbers — went to the borders of the Lake — saw several new trees but this is not the time to see plants as they are not yet out[1] / dues render similar services

---

[1] The incoherence of the text here suggests that a page may be missing from the field notebook.

not to be robbed of
everything —

At 9 A.M. we came in
sight of the ship anchored
in mouth of Rovuma
& stopped to breakfast
and wash the boats
a barracoon looking building
on left hand — 6 or 7 miles
from the sea several huts.
fish. here h send to
spread out his wings
when he seizes a large
fish in order that it
may not sink him —
the fish heads [...]
client but serving
does — with little fish
he has no diff[iculty]

= but the Africans demand simply because they have the
traveller in their power and traders accompanied by slaves
pay because they know that a panic among their attendants
is the loss of everything — the origin of the mulct is the
present which strangers give to the chief for his hospitality
which venture seems to have been diffused in the native
mind very widely — men (?) / private persons having a
village near lay claim on account of the use of their canoes
others prefer claims on most frivolous pretences as wood,
water grass

and the chiefs seeing their people enriched & no claim ever
refused makes his demand according to the means of the
traveller = traders instead of uniting against the fraud rather
side with those who have mulcted others & endeavour by
making (?) blood drinking[1] & other means to protect
themselves — it becomes at last intolerable to all & new paths
must

be resorted to in order not to be robbed of everything —
At 9 A M we came in sight of the ship anchored in mouth of
Rovuma & stopped to breakfast and wash the boats — a
barracoon looking building on left bank — 6 or 7 miles from
the sea & several huts — fish hawk said to spread out his
wings when he seizes a large fish in order that it may not
sink him

The fish hurls him about but soon dies — with little fish he
has no difficulty / in lifting him with his talons at once

---

[1] Presumably a reference to the ceremony of blood
brotherhood.

He is said to kill the large heron by lighting on & striking his head

there seems a natural antipathy between them the people say because each eats fish —

Saw ebony on right bank eight miles from sea at talus of hills that comes nearest the river

shot at hippopotamus

reached the ship at 1 P M

found all well Thanks & most hearty ones to God our gracious Preserver

no ship had called / on 10th took ship a mile up and on 11th beached her

found five small holes made in a sheet & half of copper from the coral reef at Pomony but wood sound = covered it with a sheet & half of copper some 20 feet of edge of sheathing turned down from an excessive bumping she got when we were away at end of right bank — Johanna men complained of having been treated brutally by Mr Young — knocked down & put in terror of their lives —

12th

at anchor

13th

went up about 8 miles to cut some ebony got it about $2\frac{1}{2}$ feet in diameter / and 12 feet long . . . much Pangire[1] . . . ship

[1] One of the hardwoods of the area.

108

building wood

On coming away a hippopotamus was seen waiting for us in a narrow passage 10 yards wide — went over him & he came up a few yards behind then followed and gave the boat two thumps lifting it up with ten men and about a ton of ebony in her — She was stove & when we went to beach her he followed & fortunately got a ball in his head from Dr K. He seemed a male & jealous of his herd /

14th Oct 1862

went up again to ebony hill & saw more than we have ever done — also a fine redwood = there is not more than a mile and a half of mangroves up Rovuma = they have arsenical sort of fumes when burned — saw no hippopotamus where we were attacked — The sick one has led the others off — ship sheathing put to rights and a chock in the rudder — Heard from an Arab of the coast that Mikindani point is the slaving depot station from Rovuma — They go over land to it /

15th October 1862

beached again in order to caulk under the paddle . . . This done we shall be ready to leave this = The people come down with fowls for sale regularly = writing despatches to be left at Johanna.

16th

came down to point and put wood aboard & get ready for
sea —

17th[1]

sail at 5 A.M out of Rovuma bay — rough sea & head wind =
E.S.E. sea calmer far out from land
Before leaving we told a man who was selling beautiful mats
to come again & bring the dye stuffs = He brought woods the
barks of / which are employed to dye yellow, pink & black &
was paid for them. Two new hawks = fishers speckled with a
black ring round neck.

18th

at noon we had made 130 miles & a current had carried us
southwards to opposite middle of Comoro
. . . Lat 11°33 — Long 42°22′ E at 11 30 we came in
sight of Mohilla & stopped till daybreak when we were
found to have drifted far to westward — came up to the
island anchorage at 11-30 Queen[2] sent us an ox, vegetables —
cocoanuts bananas

[1] This conflicts with the date of the 18th given in ZT
(below, p. 195).
[2] Queen of Mohilla (Moheli, in present-day usage), one of
the Comoro islands.

...cause a crack th...
...und - the ladle put in c...
allows sugar to run off
...of sheets of glass
...and a drop betw...
...when separated...

no news of any man of war having called at Johanna[1]
Rv to Molyneaux (?) 3097 sent to Cape by Mr Inglis[2] to
H.M.S. Gorgon

24th Oct 1862

she sailed at dusk=
We get six oxen from Mr Sunley at £3 = £18 = copper
sugar £28

27th Oct 1862

Engage six men at seven dollars per month — the headman
at ten D° & gave each of five £2 10 head man £4 as
2 months pay in advance=

28th Oct

scum is taken off the sugar[3] and put into a pan to settle for
night then lime is put in & it is cooled next day — The
weaker / the juice the more lime is required — It is ladled
along the different pans till it comes to the last. That is
skimmed & all scum removed lime being occasionally added
till it is of a dark yellow colour and in boiling it emits a
crackling sound — The ladle put in allows sugar to run off as
if sheets of glass and a drop between fingers when separated
& broken curls up & down slowly — It is then ready to be

[1] Blank page follows, headed by a possible Arabic Scribble.
[2] Possibly a reference to Reverend Walter Inglis.
[3] A reference to Sunley's sugar industry at Johanna.

ladled into flat wooden boxes to chrystalize & go to the turbine a centrifugal machine — If scum wont rise a banana stalk to stir it about makes it come up — If not chrystalized a shovelful of sugar / thrown in makes it chrystalize around it — If too much concentrated the chrystals dont form regularly & the sugar is damp

29th

visited the Lake at Johanna Dzealanze joined it at height of 3200 feet — probably the crater of an extinct volcano is very pretty having a peak on the West all is densely wooded around Grebes found in the Lake banks very muddy

1st Nov 1862

we wait till monday expecting the weather to settle — Prince Mahomet[B] & nephew fled here they say in fear of their lives because they are supposed to denounce slaying . . . by / between king & Mayotte[1] people = they were allowed to come on board ship by Mr Sunley's recommendation = Sidi comes round today to settle the matter = a bad case of gonorrhoea came from Mohilla for medical advice — much of this disease exists among the Mahometans

5th Nov

Before sailing this morning at 8 A M. issued an order that no man should strike any native without my orders / set off

[B] See p. 156.   [1] One of the Comoro islands.

13 NOVEMBER 1862

under steam for Mohilla at 8 A.M = sky cloudy
passed it unable to land at 3 P.M. — the surf being heavy —
saw Prince Mahomets boat close in shore — doubled back on
our course & ran our colours up to the main mast-head but
he took no notice — sky overcast & glass low

6th

at 12 had run 115 miles from Mohilla nearly west — a current
had prevented our making the southing we steered for
namely W.S.W. = we were favoured with currents and made
90 miles a day with weather against us /

11th

came in sight of fires on the land about Lindi river = coals
done could not get south further than Nyomiara found it
looking very shoal and breaking heavily — bore away for
Quillimane as the wind was fair for that —

12

steamed over the bar of Quillimane and cut wood to go up to
the village about 10 miles distant — found barque Juven
Carlotta loading with rice probably to slave /

13th

cutting wood — Saunders Wilson & Pennell[1] got leave to go

[1] The carpenter's mate and two stokers of the *Pioneer*.

ashore when we reached Quillimane and absented
themselves on 14 & 15th on morning of latter day sent for
them by King — He too remained off in a public house
drinking — In evening sent to Governor for them — some
soldiers brought them down to Col. Nunes[1] house — sent
them alone to ship but King went off again & others
followed him — next morning they were brought down / at
5-30 A.M. & came on board — Went down river after service
on 16th to be away from the village — Cut wood and on
Wednesday went with Col. Nunes
Launch over bar to H.M.S. Rapid captain Jago to take the
supplies for the missionaries

20th

came in & cut wood

22

started for Kongone & 23rd reached it early in morning —

24th

tried to catch mules — Saunders worse of liquor was abusive
& used disgusting language to Mr Young
Magrath[2] witness — sentenced him to be / on single pay and

---

[1] A Portuguese friend of Livingstone's: spelt in ZT as
Nuñez.

[2] One of the quartermasters of the *Pioneer*.

be disrated — said that he would not work again — would take
his tools and never do a bit of work again.

25th

Saunders went to his work this morning as usual — we made
a long pitfall and drove the mules over
one fell in and the other at once gave in — came & stood
quietly till a halter was put on him — took them on board
and on the 26th steamed round to Luala

27th

cutting wood — had fresh meat from Nyangalule when at
Kongone — River does not appear to have risen

30th Sunday

1st December 1862

getting wood aboard & getting ready to proceed up river /
wrote note on Map of the Viscount de Sá for Mr Frere[1]
José Nunes is with us — seventy head of cattle were sent
from Quillimane to Maruru and all died — they began to
lick the sand of the Zambesi & large balls of it were found
inside
They evidently needed salt having been accustomed to
much of it at Quillimane
remember to give ours salt occasionally —

[1] Sir Bartle Frere, Governor at Bombay.

2nd Dec 1862

went in the afternoon to look for fresh meat Dr K got two
and I one
fired into a buffalo but lost him. Hope to get away today

3rd Dec

left mouth of Luabo at 2 P.M. sleep at villages above sand of
Kongone /

4th

ran aground at Shindi island & waited for tide which now
flows far up — sleep near Expedition Island

5th

went up thence to estate Nyangombe & grounded

6th

river began to rise
Heavy rains began on night of 5th plenty of game — Dr. K.
killed 2 oryx
Large herds of buffaloes seen —

7th

water rising — hope to get up tomorrow

8th

Heaving off — Rainy
Liquid glass & gypsum chloride of alum (silicate of soda =
soluble glass) employed in embalming dead bodies
in the American war — It hardens the body into a sort
of stone

Evening meal July 10th 1862[1] 4000 . . . passed
over to the island Chusan and while marching in three
bodies to the attack of the chief city, the French bishop
Monsignore DE LA PLACE raised the city people & the
villages of the surrounding district. Even the women came
out with their bamboos & reaping knives although these
poor country people had only one fowling piece among them
which was borne in honour before the bishop but they
threw themselves upon this army of brigands killed 720 of
them, & drove the rest shamefully to their ship.

9th Dec 1862

got off yesterday
but weather very wet
lake set in rain — water . . . slowly W.Westerly /

[1] The introduction of July into a run of entries for
December 1862, may be a mistake of Livingstone's—or a
deliberate 'flash-back'. The whole passage for this entry of
July 10th 1862 is a cryptic one.

4th Dec — ... the
L.H. if admit do
was intended. But it
be well spent money to
apply for half of £300 from
Government. If that sum
is declined, then I may ask
for increase of salary on the
ground that commissioners
in the same latitudes receive
one £1000 and another £1500 per
annum. A consul lately
appointed receives £300 and
while, I get no more than
one of the lowest clerks in
the Foreign office. and it
might be urged that as I
would gain more by
writing for the press it is
scarcely fair in the Gov.t
to accept my services though
there are rendered con
amore at such a low figure

10th Dec.r tried to go
... but sound only

9th Dec 1862

the . . . L.N.[1] is almost down (done ?) . . . was intended but
it will be well spent money . . . may apply for half or £3000
from Government If that sum is declined, then I may
ask for increase of salary on the ground that commissioners
in the same Latitudes receive one £1000 & another
£1500 — per annum — A consul lately appointed receives
£700 while I get no more than one of the lowest clerks in the
Foreign Office and it might be urged that as I could gain
more by writing for the press it is scarcely fair in the Gov[t]
to accept my services though these are rendered *con amore*
at such a low figure

10th Dec

tried to go up but found only / about $5\frac{1}{2}$ feet of water
river rising — plenty of antelopes near —

11th

hear that Thornton[2] is at Senna — Stewart at Tette & one of
the mission at Shupanga.

12th

got up steam and went a few miles to be brought up again

---

[1] The *Lady Nyassa*, Livingstone's new ship, which had
been brought out in sections from Britain by Rae to be
assembled on the Zambezi; see also ZEDL, pp. 378-9.

[2] Richard Thornton, the Zambezi Expedition's mining
geologist.

beyond $\frac{1}{2}$ way tree and opposite the tree of the Gorgonites —
a huge lignum vitae 6 feet in diameter which defied all their
efforts when here with Captain Wilson[1]

13th

fresh water is well known to expand from a certain
temperature down to freezing This forms ice on the
surface This an exception to . . . law of cold contracting is
made . . . . . . / who in hearing . . . may interfere with (?) . . .
usual laws — formulae or rules of nature =

14th (Sunday) Dec 1862

The powers of the different states of the Union were
delegated to the U.S. Gov[t] in Jeffersons time so that all the
acts of the President are lawful according to the
Constitution — But that Gov[t] now suffers from the
dishonesty of her statesmen in asserting that the General
Gov[t] could not interfere in the acts of the state of Georgia
Carolina & c in shutting up black sailors belonging to
British ships — It is not believed now to have the power it
denied & is consequently now considered dishonest — The
dishonesty comes always to light / in the long run — either
now or hereafter — water falling a little — we have five feet
but that does not float us —

15th Dec 1862 — 16th

water rising — we got on and slept at Maruru

[1] Captain Wilson, R.N., of the *Gorgon*.

17th

called at Viannas and reached Shupanga found Mr Procter[1]
at Viannás =

18th

planted Gum trees at M's grave

21st

The Duckweed is used by natives up Shire as a purgative =
News from Mission very good . . . / that the Makololo had
taken charge of the country

24th Dec 1862

Still making the brasses of paddle shafts of use by turning up
and down Rains heavy

1st June is time wheat & peas — chibumba — small beans —
abobelas (?) cabbages & potatoes
Put a quantity of dry grass in a deep hole & a little earth over
it then the yam stalk and cover up — the grass rotting gives
space / for the root to expand

[1] Reverend L. J. Proctor of Bishop Mackenzie's original
party.

28th Dec 1862

went down to Viannas yesterday & came up with Mr
Procter — got seed wheat & salt — Governor-General seems
inclined to quarrel with us — by an order issued mixing us
and the mission together —

31st December 1862

Water rising very high Several prisoners sent down the day
before yesterday by Governor of Tette for speaking against
him — They are sent to be judged†

† The notebook continues without a break at this point.
The heading 1863 has been inserted to mark the new year.

Rev. J. Steward arrived about 1st Jany 1863 Mr Thornton on 2d /

4th January 1863

Moovu found guilty of stealing & must be parted with —

9th

Pioneer paddle shaft brasses finished and start up to get in the wood — paid José £22-5-4 = for goods accrued = she tows well — cut wood to make yokes & yoke legs — Slaving goes on south of Senna at Quiteve — at Gerongonzo on pretence that a few half castes and slaves are fighting with Landeens![1]: A man was sent by the head chief with two tusks to me and an offer of the whole country if I would send a few / people and drive them away — The Landeens here scouted the idea of war with them — They still receive their tribute from the Senna people — Then North of Zambesi we have Belchior and Mello and Marianno[2] and the Tette people all slaving & depopulating the country — war and alarm prevent the beneficial effects of the cruizers being realized —

[1] Zulu people.
[2] Slave raiders of African and Portuguese descent.

15th[1]

another dead body floated past us /

10th January 1863

a fact

Rae demands food and a boat separately from the Expedition or in Lady Nyassa — This is declined — said I was "cutting him off from his work by keeping out of the Lady Nyassa" I agreed to let him have his meals where he liked but could not allow the men employed for other work to work for him — We started after getting in wood above Shupanga — the Nyassa towing astern — went aground & she came into us like a battering ram — carried away a davit and nearly smashed quite the gun boat — we shall tow alongside —

12th

put L. Nyassa alongside and towed / very easily & quickly —

13th

came to mouth of Shire & took an iron house from Portuguese station there — commandant had caught a canoe of Marianno laden with powder — wine spirits & calicoes — they were going up *"in name of the missionaries"* — took in coals at Shamo & slept a mile above it. A dead body floated past

[1] Livingstone started this entry, by mistake, out of sequence, on the wrong page.

14th

came up to North end of Morambala & remain to cut wood
very showery – few people up here now – there are more
near the mouth of the river They have fled from Marianno /
Several men passed us who had been robbed of their lotos
roots and fish by his people & were naked besides – A feud
between Pidore's (?) & Marianno's people
They shoot each other when they meet

15th

another dead body floated past us – people plant only in
small patches at different spots in hopes of being able to
reap some of them – a wretched state of things

18th

Dead body got caught between ships – they are are more
than the alligators can devour & the numbers of these
animals are immense /

19th Dec

4 bodies today in reeds – one a child's – arrive at Shikan-
dakazi's village –

20th

Electric fish for sale but no fowls where formerly we got any
number
four dead bodies passed us – Rice village deserted has been
burned – we reach near Tinganes

127

Captions on drawing
Mokampata near Tinganes
residence of Marianno
Milanje range as seen from S.W. on R. Shire

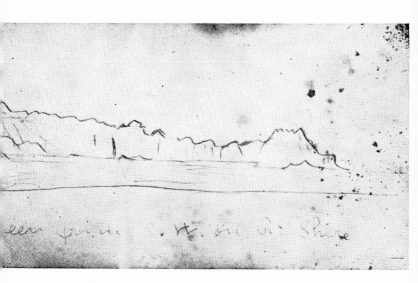

21st

Marianno is living on a small hill called Mokampata
his village is named Mochinje /

22nd

having passed by night at a very bad place for Mosquitoes
we went on Ruo to put a cross near bishop's grave. The spot
is quite flat so we could not set railings with any certainty —
a bamboo cross set up by Captain Wilson & Dr Kirk had
been taken away probably as if a fetish or charm — No one of
the mission had gone to it. It is $\frac{1}{4}$ of a mile from confluence
of Ruo down the left hand branch or at the high bank
covered with trees — two palm trees are a little beyond it

I

southwards and an acacia tree just at it / we then went up to
our wooding place at thorn trees — one of the mules plagued
by mosquitoes broke loose and fell into the fore hatchway —
had to be hauled out with tackle

23rd

Wooding — heat 99° at 3 P.M. rain during night —

24th

rains & river rising a little — hawks flying high in the
evenings live on dragon fly & moths[1] — a starving
boy we took out of charity had to be put ashore for stealing
— Kleptomania they get into a state of gnawing hunger that /
food does not satisfy

25th Sunday

= ... There are new words in the Manganja tongue about
... not found in Tette & Senna but it is essentially one
language

26th

a bank formed at an island having an innumerable flock of
birds on it kept us all day fast — L. Nyassa grounded & we
had to cast her off to get clear ourselves
In thinking of success people cannot realize the worry that

[1] Written over the text here is a barely decipherable
drawing captioned 'Toe with Knobs like Swifts'.

the head of the expedition has to endure from the /
carelessness & selfishness — of underlings
an engineer taking the pet or neglecting his work — or
playing when he ought to be working — sickness made most
of

29th January 1863

drifted on during night more firmly — another body floated
past making nineteen in all — many went past no doubt
unseen by us
How much more evil has the Almighty for me
with her and them I have had to bear from my fellow
creatures let me think this and be / patient
Johnstone the black cook of the mission came down in the
afternoon and told us of the death by fever of poor dear
Scudamore[1] Acetate of lead seems to relieve the vomiting
what shall we say and what shall we speak

1st February 1863

We have been a whole week hauling one vessel after another
when Pioneer touches a bank is formed at once & impossible
to haul her over — not noticing this we lost much time —
Magrath guilty of impertinence /

[1] Reverend H. C. Scudamore of the U.M.C.A. party; see
cha., *passim.*

...v Newell of your
language — But your
... to live a
real christian life
amidst all th worry
& cares of our condit
Let the heart be
fixed resting on
the Lord & try to act
as He may He
supposed would
have done in like
position — Put the
disagreeables in the
most favourable
light & them ...
... pleasant ...
against the bitter
... our serious
... ... taken

& Newell of foul language — to Mr Young
How to live a real Christian life amidst all the worry & cares
of our condition
Let the heart be fixed resting on the Lord & try to act as he
may be supposed would have done in like position — Put the
disagreeables in the most favourable light & then the sweet
or pleasant ones against the bitter & hope that our service
may be acceptable to the Master above /

2nd February 1863

came to first sharp bend & failed first day when our engines
failed us

3rd

tried & failed . . . warped through came to by sharp bend
with boiling . . . that throws steering quite out —

5th

failed —

6th

hauled her through first part and failed by an off running
branch sucking us with it. Wilson jaundiced
Saunders ill —

6th

laid out an anchor haul her past the branch that
complicated the bend — hauled up Nyassa grounded threw
her off then / *got her up = to late to steam*
wild ducks laying now

7th

coal our last resource nearly gone
went on in hopes of getting up to more wood
stuck at round bend & lost half a day — boat upset by
splashing paddles
hippo shot afloat /

Caption on drawing
Sunday 8 February 1863

9th February 1863

passed . . . island & make (?) two paddle floats — was whole
day getting through — got past No 7 bend

10th

no passage at a . . . . . . whole day there

11th

passage opened by night — took a canoe — and went up a
quarter of a mile — no passage
went across a mile of deep marsh of foul smell to palm trees
— saw a few wretches eking out life with palm seed, & palm

135

wine — a young bird brought in just out of egg shell roasted
and divided — one man seemed dying a skeleton gave a yard
of calico / & they sent up a palm tree and drew some wine
for us — said if we had come at proper time they could have
made us all drunk

13th

remove her up a little — Rains
Fire flies flash sumultaneously & make a beautiful lightning
gleam over the tops of the tall grasses

14

Patience patience
river rising a little

15th

D° D° D° cold fogs began today

16th

dragging vessel /

17th

Mr Waller came down in Thornton's boat to visit us — the

Makololo have been behaving ill

18th

Mr Proctor arrived from below with canoes

19th

Procter & Waller[1] leave a number of the bird
scopus was killed & found very fat which fat is strong
tasted — They have a long rounded bill with a sulcus
between the upper & lower mandible — the knobnosed
goose or servic (?) live on grass seeds just now — they come
to sand bank to swallow stones to assist digestion — one
breathed by his humerus drought has been severe / & so
has famine in consequence —

20th

we got a waterbuck by C.L. — men cutting wood — &
dragging ship —

21st

cloudy & rainy a hippo shot by C L. & secured —

[1] Horace Waller, originally lay superintendent of the
U.M.C.A. party; subsequently ordained in the Church of
England; a passionate anti-slavery pamphleteer and editor of
Livingstone's *Last Journals*.

22nd

got Pioneer over this morning — Alligators very numerous
here
They tear a dead body to pieces in a short time pulling up
their heads to swallow
When one begins to splash all the others rush to spot —
Wilson better — The only thing to occupy the minds of the
crew is shooting / and skinning and the hooking alligators or
rather crockodiles
a large short snouted black fellow seems to be the animal of
the Nile

24th February 1863

hauling the Lady Nyassa through a . . . shot —

1st March

nearly through

2nd

hauling place at island where we wooded

3rd

came up to the end of palm grove and cut wood

138

4th

had to haul again in consequence of Nyassa being /
alongside — water rising

5th

went about a mile & were brought up again at $4\frac{1}{2}$ feet
warping — hippo shot by Dr K.
birds have marrow in the Tibiae

6th

3 Hippos shot by C.L. 2 came down to us —

9th

still hauling vessels

10th

got up $\frac{1}{2}$ a mile when crossing above Tura island
L Nyassa grounded & parted all fasteners

11th

got up to / near Ebony wooding place & canoed asternd still
again

12th

went & cut a block of ebony for capstan saw one Lignum
vitae tree — country very dry

13th

got the L Nyassa afloat — Shupangamen men sold all meat of
Hippopotamus to the Manganja for hoes — then denied all —
saying there was no fat

14th

shot a crockodile

15th

water rising and rain on hills & at ship — /
fourth or canine tooth secured with a socket in upper jaw
Alligator with a . . . here front teeth come through Alligator
has not webbed hind foot of crockodile four toes front foot
five but not webbed as in hind foot /

16th March 1863

a letter came down at . . . A M from Waller saying that
Dickinson[1] & Clarke[2] were very ill

[1] Dr John Dickinson, medical officer of the U.M.C.A. party.
[2] Artisan (shoemaker) member of the U.M.C.A. party.

the former jaundiced
the latter having violent epileptic seizures
Dr K & I got out the whaler & set off – slept at
Mankokwes –

1 7th

set off at 7 A M
rested a $\frac{1}{4}$ hour at the high bank below mission sun being
very hot – reached the mission at 5 saw Waller coming
down to us weeping
Dr Dickinson had expired 10 minutes before in a fainting
fit had passed / no urine for some days – constant vomiting
had prevented any medicine being retained except calomel
& he was salivated – no urine passed for many days but no
coma supervened – large quantities of bile were ejected – a
seidlitz powder caused a slight motion of the bowels – He
had an inveterate disinclination to taking calomel – had
fever constantly
was very weakly one lung being gone ought to have left / the
country and had determined to do so but then resolved to
brave it – a very lovely and deeply religious character
He was quite sensible and asked Procter to pray with him –
a fainting fit came on
a dose of chloric then revived him & another dose being
offered he said – "I cant" & expired – A great loss – but he by
whose Providence it happened knows what is best for His
own cause
We buried him beside / Dear Scudamore

They feel the loss greatly & so will all who knew him

19th

The water having come down with a rise of 4 inches I
started this morning for the ship called at Mankokwés &
then reached home by 9 P M taking her through after
wooding all well
This my wife said last year is my birth day — The Good
Lord make me useful as he favours me (?) / on the 18th
Chibisa's son came to see me
his father was killed by Terero or (?) Mello
and he has come to live at the old place near Dakanamoio
island — Told him that God saw the deeds of men & had
seen how his father had helped the slave hunters & those
whom he had help to destroy others had killed himself
Sent for the Makololo
They came and on enquiry I found that they had a very
plausible / story to tell — they admitted that they had taken
wives from the Ajawa because the Manganja refused to
marry naked people — That they had fought with Mañkokwe
because when they went down to hunt elephants he
demanded who had told them about *his* elephants and
would they give him the under half of all they killed — I
suppose that the answer was unacceptable (?) because
arrows / shot at them and two wounded
This is partly true for today when Mankokwe brought the
Makololo subject forward I said it would be better to make

143

your statement face to face with the accused for they too
have a grievance against you — you shot at them and
wounded them with your arrows — at which he burst into a
laugh and was joined by all present

Moloka — /

Ramakukana & Malaori (?) went down on another occasion
to hunt — attacked a cow elephant and her calf — Moloka was
caught and tusks pierced his leg arm chest and back under
the scapula — from this last wound air escaped as he
breathed — (He is now completely shattered) — He was made
insensible and the animal left him after standing a while over
his limp / body — She & the calf were killed and then they
heard by his call that he had revived They gave cow & calf
to Mañkokwe & told him to send men up to the mission at
. . . and they got assistance by a canoe — The missionary
carried him up & took care of him — They very cleverly
concentrated on what they had done for the bishop &
Burrup[1] especially the latter

then for a wonder without adverting to the war to which the
bishop led them / at Monasomba's

they mentioned their good conduct up at the Mazitu
country at the Lake — They challenged proof of their having
killed so many people and said that Chibisa's people had
been the guilty ones and the missionaries admit that this is
partly true — I told them that I did not disapprove of what
they had done in dispersing the slave hunters

---

[1] Reverend Henry de Wint Burrup of the U.M.C.A.; see
cha., *passim.*

144

They say that they offered the three bales of calico to the /
missionaries but these were declined

This too is true — on hearing both sides and taking about
half as true on each side

I come to the conclusion that both Manganja and Makololo
have been guilty of much wrong — and one is as bad as the
other

The Makololo might have been utilized but the Manganja
are like silk purses and sows ears — The Ajawa with / the
Makololo have plundered a great deal & many have been
driven away by them for so doing

some of these fled to the mission and the missionaries
account of them tallies exactly with what is said by the
Makololo

away from the earth Wilson 626[1]

Akari 1/6 (Malati) . . . Madzokombo 3 fathoms for 3 years
Abdulla 2/6 /

sick five weeks Dec & January — again

---

[1] The following three lines are written upside down in
the notebook. For the last seventeen pages of the notebook
Livingstone appears to have written all his entries hap-
hazardly, often in reverse sequence to those in other sections.

sick four weeks
Dec. & January – again
Q.M. Feb 7 Off sick list
13th

The effort of the English
Gov.t is worthy of all
praise – Had it not
been for these I especially
of those of England Africa
as yet had scarcely
been accessible to
missionary labour
It is devoutly to be
hoped that this noble
and disinterested
... may not
... until this

9th Feb

off sick list

13th

the effort of the English Gov^t is worthy of all praise – Had it
not been for these & especially of those of England Africa as
yet had scarcely been accessible to missionary labour & it is
devoutly to be hoped that these noble and disinterested
measures may not be relaxed until this foul demon be
chased away (?) / on arriving (?) – out cattle-carts – waggon
and things that will not spoil to be collected in one spot
ashore & covered
all spoilable things to be put aboard Pioneer under awnings
& covered – iron house – food tent to form first load – picks
& spades – axes – theodolites
lucifers – cooking utensils
seruka

      Tekterka   Zambesi

2nd February

Drayman $\frac{1}{2}$ a dollar for $1\frac{1}{2}$ fathom
Bakari & Jimu (?) 1 piece between them 10/-

3rd February 1863

/ Zachariah 1 piece of calico — 18 January 10/-
Molungo[1] a da funa panzipioma da pasa muana ache bura
eka mbami a nno tsiwa a si saika nanane moro a kale kale —

— *a the* create

= Kuanga

Mbono Mboio name of Reed buck M

    chitoñkoro   only

    brother

    funika chipanga (?) /

acquire the art of exerting an influence over heathen minds
— to reduce unwritten barbarous language to call into
exercise energies that have slumbered for centuries and to
endure patiently the reverses — trials & disappointments
incident to missionary life — This requires the best and
ablest men the church can furnish /

teachers — 39 schools one Grammar & one
superior school[2]

missionaries ought to be men of high moral & intellectual
attainments — of tried & undoubted piety — ought to have
the capacity to exert a commanding influence in their native
country

[1] This passage which is heavily overwritten and altered in
the original represents, presumably, an attempt by
Livingstone to transcribe the local speech. It seems to be a
statement on God's relations with His creatures.

[2] 'teachers ... School': these two lines clearly belong
after '88 native ...' at head of p. 151.

mental energy & thorough piety — to look into all windings
and intricacies of heathen character
habits (?) feelings & motives of men who have
sympathies . . . . . . /

Chimoasa	9th Jan	
Joangezi	1863	
Kanyai		
Joangeti		
Bakari		Kasa = kindle
Manoel		Chipanupanu = firefly
Asangano		Kheidzi — frog that whistles
Bisenti		
Dasinto		
Afasi		

. . . water ordeal.[1]

---

[1] This page concludes with three indecipherable lines.

In 1855 the church missions in West had 3354
communicants 88 native /
de 1862 da idade 41[1]
Fight for slaving still going on — 2d men going out —
Sunley — but will free trade be given to parts not
interfering with their territories — stimulus to their trade &
possessions —
Chisara or Patricio

28th Dec 1862

other
a few days previously /
Remainder wheat from Vianna
potatoes & figs from Quillimane & Cape — Rum for men —
Dorminda aqui esta M M L em Esperanca da resurrecciao e
felicidade pelo Nosso Salvador Jesus Christus[2]

Repouzao   restos
Aqui restao . . . os restos mortaes de M ML
em esperanca da resurreicao e felicidade pelo
Nosso Salvador Jesus Christus
Fallicida a 27 Abril /
    Southsea =
Portsmouth Dockyard

[1] Reference to Mary Moffat Livingstone's age at her death;
the accompanying sketches seem to be designs for her
gravestone.

[2] This appears to be an attempt by Livingstone to work out
in Portuguese an inscription for his wife's gravestone (see
page 41).

28 DECEMBER 1862

£5 Mrs Pearce 46 Albion St Brighton Sussex   Coast
Guard[1]
Newell to have a second good conduct stripe
Gondo thick native cloth
Ngonda = a rag or covering
Tamatave Lat 18° 16.1 Antananarivo 18 56′ 26″ S
Long. Tamatave 49° 28.5
capital 47 57 48′ /

£10 to Mrs Collyer 13 Bilbury St. Plymouth to be payable at
Devonport Dockyard

£10 to Mrs Magrath Dawlish Devonshire
8th Dec 1862

£5 to Sarah Jane Saunders – 16 Plymouth St /
Mikindani point is slaving station
Length of tube 14 ft Diameter 24 ins Diameter of water 13
in Speed 4 seconds

When rains begin with full moons they come with storms &
very much of it – are called bad seasons but with quarters
the opposite – Portuguese observation

---

[1] This and similar notes following appear to be references
to payments to members of the *Pioneer*'s crew and their
dependents.

$$
\begin{array}{ll}
60 & \ 210 \\
14 & \Big)\ \ 60 \\
\hline
240 & 3\,)12600 \\
60 & \quad 4200 \\
\hline
4\,)840 \\
\ \ 210
\end{array}
$$

/

drawing 18 inches while Pioneer does for Shire —
If Englishmen establish themselves on Lake N — they will
prefer the Rovuma with all its difficulties to paying tribute
to the Portuguese which would be virtually acknowledging
their right to blocade the mouths of the rivers
Due to Johanna men £117-8-
Oct Advance £2-16 to . . . & £4 to head man / [1]

. . . — . . .
Mekunde = deep = meai — . . .
Chirimbodi = yam
Matingi pumpkins
Mkogo = cassava
Louma — Rive Rovuma
Kwahao = waterfalls
15th Lat 10 53 45
       Long 39 40 30
Kokojamani island
maduka instead of Madzuka days = mangalo — rocks
(msaka a married man) (upare = batchelor — same
Panijela = man from whom we brought wood
Banijira = young batchelor
Bawene = yonder Mbero Do No

[1] A page has been torn or cut out here.

ea
Tasianduri behind / 1 40 + G. di F — Rate Zurima (. . .
Long — 40 30 E Rovuma

              anchorage

Lat. 10 28 30

Chidia Lake

Tombama shoat (?) arirma such

pasembo give me

12th Sept 1862 Lat in

10° 48′ 20″

10   28   30   Rovuma
_____

    19   50

      12th sept 1862

        Longitude   39° 55

                  40 30
                         _____

                       35   Westing /

. . .   180

Potatoes   146
               ___

         326 —   13

Eggs 10 doz —   5

10   milk   5

meat   18

      35
      ___

      53 —   10 —

2 doz fowls   8
                     ___

To Alli wa Omar   41

    154

Those people who have passed away have gained by what
they did & we shall have a gain by what we do = *Koran*

12	17	Mohilla
43	46	Torren (?)
		anchorage

*This uncaptioned drawing of hills faces the
page of the notebook which ends '210' (p. 153). It is
placed here as an appropriately mysterious
tailpiece to conclude the cryptic and
disorganized last seventeen pages
of Livingstone's entries.*

^A In ZT (below, p. 180), Livingstone excused the employment of slave labour by the British consul at Johanna as an economic necessity: so also did Captain Gardner of the *Orestes* (below, p. 169). In a reference, however, in 1850 to Rae's prospective employment in Sunley's sugar industry, Horace Waller of the Universities' Mission was less charitable: '. . . the slaves do the work, English find the money, no questions asked and Vivat Regina! Poor Africans!' (ZJJS, p. 241).

^B A cryptic and only partially decipherable passage. Some light is thrown on it in a letter by Livingstone to his daughter, Agnes, of 18 December 1862: 'In coming back two men of Johanna, one called Prince Mahomet — a gentleman — and the other Abadoo, a fellow educated by the missionaries at Bombay, had formerly gone about various parts, begging, as "a Colonel of the Army of Johanna". He was, I believe, baptized, but is now a Mohamedan and had prevailed on the other man to flee with him as if in danger of his life by the King of Johanna. They came on board the Pioneer for protection, but the consul said there was no necessity: Abadoo was only making a tool of him. So I told them to go to the consul's house. They got into their small boat and went off to Mohilla, and may go to Mauritius, or England, if they can. Of those educated by missionaries some turn out well, other (*sic*) receive all the temporal advantages of education and turn it all to evil.' (ZEDL, p. 226.)

156

Livingstone's Rovuma Despatches of 1862

TO EARL RUSSELL

THE FOLLOWING DESPATCHES from David Livingstone to the British Foreign Secretary, Earl Russell, give
Livingstone's official account of his Rovuma expedition of
1862. They are taken from copies in the *Zambesi Expedition
Journal* (pages 93 and 99-106) at the Livingstone Memorial,
Blantyre, Scotland, and are not reproduced in J. P. R.
Wallis's edition, *The Zambezi Expedition of David Livingstone, 1858-1863* (London, 1956). Forms of address have
been removed.

No. 4.   Johanna, 2 September 1862.

After launching the vessel for Lake Nyassa at Shupanga
it was necessary to go down to the sea for provisions in
doing which we found the river so much fuller that it
appeared better to proceed to this island with the Johanna
crew whose period of service had expired, and spend the
months between this and the December flood of the Zambesi in boat exploration of the Rovuma, than in slowly
wending our way up the Shire, and probably being
obliged to wait at some point for the rams. Our object in
going to the Rovuma is if possible to find an outlet of our
own away from the Portuguese to the large and well
peopled tract (Livingstone's deletion) region bathed by
the waters of Lake Nyassa. The inveterate slave hunting
of the African, Portuguese cases of which I have lately
laid before your Lordship and the disinclination of the
statesmen of Lisbon to allow free trade on the Zambesi
sufficiently explain my anxiety to have an opening into
the countries for lawful commerce beyond their control.

    We came to Johanna in seventeen days and intend
starting for the Rovuma in a day or two.

    158

No. 5.   Rovuma Bay, 16 October 1862.

By the kindness of Capt. Gardner we were towed from Johanna to this bay by H.M.S. Orestes and commenced the ascent of the Rovuma River in two boats on the 9th September. This being the dry season and the water said to be unusually low the navigation even in boats was difficult. The stream crosses from side to side in a sandy channel three quarters of a mile wide, and at these crossings or when the water was divided into three or four portions we had generally to drag the boats about fifty or a hundred yards. The influence of the tide is not observed more than two miles from the mouth. There are not more than two miles of Mangroves in consequence and at about six miles from the sea the highlands begin. These highlands look like ranges of hills on each side of the river. Their spurs sometimes come down to the water's edge, yet often leave a mile of rich level alluvial soil between the slopes and the banks. The slopes are thickly covered with brushwood and trees, and it being our winter the landscape was of a light gray colour dotted over with spots of green where certain trees had preceded the rest in putting on new foliage. On ascending to the top of the slopes they were found to be only the edges of a thickly wooded table land on which many bamboos showed a somewhat humid climate and considerable patches of cultivation indicated the industry of the inhabitants. The channel to which the river is confined in floods is very straight and has a direction about West South West, the plateau continues to lend beauty and an appearance of healthiness to both banks of the river for about 80 miles. Then retires and leaves a widely extended plain in front dotted over with detached granitic hills. In that plain rocks begin to appear in the river and at the point beyond which it would have been imprudent to push the boats the entire bed was rocky and the water flowed between masses of stones four or five feet high by numerous channels. Through these the native canoes pass with ease for there is a great deal of trade carried out in rice and salt. We could have hauled our boats through but the channels further up were reported to be still more narrow and it was nearly certain that in the descent we should share the fate of some whom tradition reports to have tried to bring a load of slaves down these cataracts.

Unlike any other cataracts we have seen the land on the bank is perfectly level and free from rock and as far as the eye could reach in front the country was level with detached hills one of which was conical and probably igneous, for pieces of coal which the natives knew would burn were found in the sands of the Rovuma and we have seen that the coals elsewhere in this country have all been brought to the surface by igneous action. Our turning point about a mile below an island Nyamitolo was in latitude 11° 13′ 30″ South and longitude 38° 39′ East that is assuming the Longitude of the anchorage in this bay to be 40° 3′ E. We were then about one hundred and fourteen miles in a straight line from the coast or by Long. & Lat. together to give a fair idea of the distance we had come one hundred and fifty six miles up the river.

From the natives we learned that our turning point the small cataract Chimbarabara was about thirty miles below the confluence of another river called Niende or Liende with the Rovuma. It is said to arise in the mountains in the Eastern shores of Lake Nyassa, it is very broad but at this season the water is only ankle deep. The country around the confluence named Ngomano is under the chief Ndonde and there the slave route from Quiloa (Kilwa) to Nyassa crosses the Rovuma. The only motive to travel these thirty miles on foot would have been to make the acquaintance and give a present to Ndonde of whom I have vague impressions that he assisted to bring the murderers of Mr. Roscher to justice but I know nothing positively.

At Michi three or four days further down the river we were actually upon another part of the slave route named —but even then indirect enquiry elicited no information.

An intelligent chief there who had visited the coast and

knew the different races of whites said positively, "You English are the first white men we ever saw up here" so poor Roscher must have identified himself in dress with the Arabs and left no traces of his own individuality in the country.

It may be interesting to geographers to know that Ngomano is reported to be two Arab days from the Lake by their usual route parallel to the Liende, and the Rovuma flows from the West in a narrow rocky channel fit only for canoes. It is still asserted to come out of Lake Nyassa but by a narrow passage and down precipices. As Roscher probably crossed the river at Ngomano the object of his last fatal trip may have been to examine it at its upper end. Near the coast the people are degenerate half caste Arabs who cultivate a little and occasionally eke out their earnings by slaving. Mikindany is reported to be the point of export.

Further up we have the native tribe Makonde on the North and Mabiha on the South. The chief difference between the two is that the Mabiha men as well as women wear the hideous lip ring. The language is of the same class as the Zambesi dialects but much more guttural. The Makonde were friendly until we had ascended about sixty miles. We then found them to be regular river pirates living in sand banks they said for fear of being stolen and intent we thought on stealing others. We were pressed to land at one village where two human heads had been cut off but civilly declined as one would an invitation from the common hangman. Many of them however came about us afterwards and exhibited curiosity alone. They subsequently followed the boats till they came to a high bank overlooking a narrow passage and commenced without the smallest provocation shooting at us with their arrows. Though quite within range of their muskets we stopped and expostulated as well as we could and while doing so even allowed some to come on a sand bank behind us with their arrows. We were determined to spare no effort to avoid a collision, and to some who were induced to come unarmed to one of the boats the superiority of our arms was explained and our great desire for friendship rather than using them.

They had no reason for their conduct but "White men never went up this river and you shan't either". We even distributed about thirty yards of calico as tokens of friendship and moving on in the belief that all was right we received a volley of arrows and musket balls, four of the latter passing through the boat sail at which the long palaver took place. After doing this they bolted back among the reeds and bushes with which the high bank was covered probably expecting that we should be thrown into confusion by some being killed and they might then plunder all the boats contained. They made no attempt to stand and return fire but ran away keeping as well as they could out of sight. In our descent we passed through all these people without the least molestation. Higher up we found the people of the same tribe very friendly, laying down their arms generally before coming near the boats: and beyond the unfriendly borderers a great deal of trade is carried out by means of canoes. Seven canoes accompanied us for three days and were found laden with salt which the Makua and Makonde extract from the soil. Above Ngomano a large tract of country is reported destitute of human inhabitants but abounding in game and above this very friendly tribes engaged in making salt.

The danger to which treachery by those who did not know the English might have exposed us, confined our observation almost entirely to the banks. As in the Shire and elsewhere more than one visit is necessary to gain the confidence of the natives. We are sure that the general feeling must be in our favour and any other expedition will be more at liberty to examine the country.

All we saw of the land seemed fertile and with the exception alluded to the inhabitants were friendly and industrious. Food was abundant but a sense of insecurity was apparent for while the people had villages on land they preferred to live on sand banks while the river was low. Large quantities of grain were stored away in the woods but they seemed less anxious about that than about themselves. The oil yielding seed Sesame which is largely exported from Mozambique to France is produced in large quantities and a great deal of honey is secured by hives placed on trees. Cotton is cultivated but we did not see much. Gum copal is found and is probably collected for the Zanzibar market. In addition to these articles of trade the Rovuma is famous for ebony. There it attains a size seldom seen in commerce. A wood called on the Zambesi "Pangire" is well adapted for ship building and many other woods quite new to us would probably be valuable in trade.

The enclosed tracing[1] of the river was made by Dr. Kirk and gives a good idea of all we saw above the point reached by the Rovuma in 1861. The sketches of the Rovuma and Liende above our turning point are from native information but reliable.

Having now visited this river in flood and at its lowest ebb it is probable that a lucrative trade might be developed on it by a steamer drawing when loaded only eighteen inches of water. The people seem willing to cultivate for sale and as they might be visited several times during the seven or eight months of the year when the navigation is open, the goods now carried from the Lake region to Kilwa and Ibo would take advantage of a market so much more near the interior as Michi or the first cataract. The Rovuma has tsetse & snags but no bar and the country looked healthy though we had a little fever among us, and should English trade flourish on the Lake this route with any disadvantages it may possess will be preferred to paying dues to our allies who have established a sort of paper blockade at the mouth of the Zambesi.

P.S. At Johanna. 21 October 1862.

We sailed from the Rovuma on the 17th and after spending a day at Mohilla reached Pomony bay yesterday. We coal and provision here as quickly as possible and after

[1] Not available at LMB: presumably, this is in the Public Record Office, London.

shipping six draught oxen from Mr. Sunley we shall proceed at once back to the Zambesi.

We are glad to find that we have performed the Rovuma service during the very time that our progress would have been hindered on the Shire by low water. As the flood begins in November no time has been lost.

We received every assistance from H.M. Consul Wm. Sunley Esq. who does everything in his power to forward this work.

Extract from the Logbook of
H.M.S. 'Orestes'

3 SEPTEMBER 1861 TO 5 JUNE 1865

Page from the 'Orestes' logbook, showing entries
(Sept. 5th and 6th) referring to Livingstone.

THE FOLLOWING EXTRACTS from the journal at the front of this logbook (now in the possession of the Livingstone Memorial, Blantyre, Lanarkshire) add further details to the brief description given by Livingstone in *The Zambesi and its Tributaries* (see pages 180 to 204 below) of the association between him and Captain Gardner, R.N., commander of the British naval squadron off the East African coast.

When Livingstone wrote to his brother, Tom, at the end of his exploration of the Rovuma in boats in 1862, he described the services which Gardner and the *Orestes* had given to his party

The Orestes, a fine big Man of war with 21 68-pounder guns, came to Johanna as we were about to leave for this coast, and Captain Gardner very kindly offered to tow us over and thereby save our coals for our return. She walked along with the Pioneer as if she had nothing behind her— Up and down over huge waves, for it blew very fresh. Poor little Pioneer had to tumble and tear along till, snap went a cable as thick as your thigh, and we had to get up steam on our own hook and soon came to this Bay. Captain Gardner went up with us for two days to see us fairly started.[1]

In a letter written at the same time to his daughter, Agnes, Livingstone noted, 'Captain Gardner went up with us about 30 miles and he remarked how much more promising a field for missions this river presented than the west coast. It is more healthy looking by far, but there is a good time coming yet for Eastern as well as for Western Africa, and it may please God to make us pioneers for his great work'.[2] These remarks not only illuminate Livingstone's missionary ambitions for the Rovuma; they also indicate—as is apparent from page 175 below—the friendly relations which existed at that time between Gardner and Livingstone. At the end of the Zambezi Expedition, however, relations between the two men were much less cordial. The *Orestes* had towed the

[1] ZEDL, p. 217.   [2] Ibid, p. 220.

Pioneer from the Zambezi to Mozambique and Living-stone had handed the vessel over to the Navy. Three of its crew decided to remain with him and, in his words, 'Gardner did not act as fairly as he might have done and extracted a promise from me in writing to pay the men's wages, who having been with me for years, volunteered to see me safe to Bombay. I strove to avoid a quarrel, but he was decidedly impudent and bullying.'[1]

In these extracts, Gardner's spellings of *Rovuma* and *Rae* have been regularized and his punctuation has been corrected occasionally.

[1] ZEDL, p. 387.

September 2. Noon. Saw a small steamer at anchor in Pomony which turned out to be the Pioneer, Dr. Livingstone's exploring vessel with that Gentleman, his brother, Dr. Kirk and Mr. Rae the Engineer on board.

We got into Pomony very well though it was blowing strong and a heavy sea running and the natives thought we should not attempt it. Mohamed Ali came to me afterwards and said I must have a strong heart to bring so large a ship into so small a port on such a day. I learnt from Sidi Drayman that the King was at Pomony having come round from Johanna in the Pioneer. Dr. Livingstone and Dr. Kirk came aboard and dined with us—they had been some days on the island having come up from the Zambesi and were going on to explore the Rovuma. As I intended to go on to Zanzibar I offered to tow the Pioneer to the Rovuma which Dr. Livingstone gladly accepted.

Pomony is a wretched place for a depot besides being unhealthy, and I was glad to get out of it as soon as possible. We took in some provisions and stripped the remaining copper off the Veya the Consul having taken off part, although nearly $1\frac{1}{2}$ tons have been taken from her and packed up in cask. She is high up on the beach but is bildged.

Mr. Sunley is hard at work making his sugar and seems to be going on very prosperously, the sugar cane coming at a great pace. I was surprised to see how ably and intelligently the blacks (mostly slaves) do their allotted tasks. They drive the engine, make the waggons, break in cattle for draught and drive them and conduct all the different operations without any white overlooker besides Mr. Sunley. As the King was anxious to return to Johanna in the Orestes instead of going in his boats I invited him to go round with me and he came on board at the hour I named 8 o'clock on the morning of the 5th.

5th

Unfortunately he was caught in a storm and with his party four of whom were women got very wet, and I had to make them as comfortable as I could in my cabin. The state of the weather prevented our weighing at the time I had named and we could not get out until the afternoon, in the meantime the King amused himself in my cabin. I played him a couple of games of chess, one of which he won cleverly enough. We took the Pioneer in tow, and ran round the island under sail, putting the King and his party into boats about a mile and a half from the town; it was labouring hard and they must have had a nasty pull to get home, the squalls coming down very heavy off the land, one of which split the main topsail—after landing His M[ajesty] off Johanna we bore up for the Rovuma with Pioneer in tow steering to leeward of Comoro. Breeze very fresh and much sea on. Kept under easy sail and took the Pioneer along 7 knots. Strong current setting us NW.

7th

Sunday. We had kept under very cosy sail during the night but made rather too much at daylight, and carried away both hawsers. The Pioneer then went on with her own engines. Running into Rovuma bay during church and anchored off the mouth of the river a little before noon. Pioneer got in half an hour after us. I invited Dr. Livingstone to take a run up the river in my boat and to dine with me afterwards. Mr. Playfair accompanied us. We took the last of the flood and got up to a village on the left bank about 8 miles distant from the ship, then came down with the first of the ebb, accomplishing the whole in about three hours.

Like the river Teign in old Devonshire the Rovuma presents at high water a large expanse but in the present dry season when the tide is out it shrivels into a few channels between high sand banks which are intricate and hardly allow the passage of a boat. But on this our first occasion of observing the river it looked very respectable.

8th

Wishing to see a little more of the river and to send Dr. Livingstone rejoicing on his way, I determined to accompany him for two days run and to return on the third, and in order to give some of the officers a due opportunity of seeing something of the interior to take one of the cutters in addition to the galley.

Sept 9th

We made all our preparations on Monday and left the ships on Tuesday at 10.30 A.M., a little before low water. The flood came in later than we expected. The boats were repeatedly aground and we did not reach the village which we had got to on Sunday until 2.30 P.M.—but then we were delayed by falling in with a herd of hippopotami which occupied us more than half an hour; When we first saw them their backs were out of water but on the approach of the boats they disappeared, but showed their heads every now and then above water to blow and breath. I was astonished at the enormous size of these heads which very much resembled that of the horse. I struck one in the centre of the forehead and one or two other balls took effect, but with what results to the great beasts we could not judge as they retired to their sub-aqueous homes.

The cutter was a great drag to us and I would have sent her back to the ship only that it would have been a great disappointment to the officers in her and she carried Mrs. Tracy, Gorges and Blackman. In the galley I had Mr. Playfair and Dr. Livingstone as a visitor. In the two boats belonging to the expedition were Dr. Kirk, Mr. Livingstone, and Mr. Rae (who however being ill with dysentery returned with us), Collier Quarter Master and Newall AB belonging to this ship lent by me for the exup the river Ruvooma

were made up of Zambesi and other black natives, one of the former a very fine specimen of a man. —

After lunching at our first stopping place we pushed on again until dark, during which time we did not make more than five or six miles in consequence of the boats being so frequently aground, in fact the cutter had to be carried a great part of the way

We bivouacked on a flat sand raised a few feet above the river with thick bush in the rear but no stagnant water and no musquitoes, we made tents with our awnings on shore at least Dr. Livingstone and I did and the following night the cutter followed our example — I wished much for the painters' art to be able to catch the strikingly beautiful scene of our moonlight encampment, the still expanse of water around us, the placid night, moon nearly at the full, and the sky bright with stars, the thick bush in the background with large trees and a great fire going up with a dense smoke made by the natives for clearing the land or perhaps by accident — three large cooking fires (sailors delight in making them as large as possible) with the men cooking, officers reclining in every possible attitude, (ordinary Englishmen accustomed to table and chairs do not know how to recline and cannot get their legs under them) a candle, with a board to windward to keep it from flaring, throwing a strong light on our supper. I never saw such Chiaro Scu

Page from Captain Gardner's journal.

pedition, and a man named Perse a Q Master belonging to it—their crews were made up of Zambesi and other black natives, one of the former a very fine specimen of a man.

After lunching at our first stopping place we pushed on again until dark, during which time we did not make more than five or six miles in consequence of the boats being so frequently aground, in fact the cutter had to be carried a great part of the way.

We bivouacked on a flat sand raised a few feet above the river with thick bush in the rear but no stagnant water and no mosquitoes. We made tents with our awnings on shore, at least Dr. Livingstone and I did and the following night the cutter followed our example. I wished much for the painters art to be able to catch the strikingly beautiful scene of our moonlight encampment, the still expanse of water around us, the placid night, moon nearly at the full, and the sky bright with stars, the thick bush in the background with large trees and a great fire going up with a dense smoke made by the natives for clearing the land or perhaps by accident. Three large cooking fires (sailors delight in making them as large as possible / with the men cooking, officers reclining in every possible attitude (ordinary Englishmen accustomed to tables and chairs do not know how to recline and cannot get their legs under them) a candle, with a board to windward to keep it from flaring, throwing a strong light on our supper. I never saw such Chiaroscuro. It would have delighted an artist.

I had taken my hammock which was slung along the ridge of our tent and in which I slept as comfortably as I should have done on board, between sheets and blankets and with a good pillow. The men were well protected and covered, yet I heard several of them complain of cold in the morning but nobody had a single mosquito bite, at least none of our party, but strange to say the old campaigners were bitten.

Sounded the Reveille at 5 A.M. A cup of tea and off again morning at first misty—passed several very shallow places, had to get assistance to carry the galley over one. Stopped to breakfast at 8, to dine at one, and finally bivouacked at the foot of a hill at 4.30 P.M. spreading our tents on the sand bank.

We made about 14 miles this day and the place we arrived at was within a mile of the spot reached by Dr. Livingstone in the Pioneer towards the end of the rainy season two or three years back when the river was full. We were close to the left bank which at this place rose a couple of hundred feet which we ascended to get a view of the lake on the other side which probably joins the river when the latter is at its full. We passed several hamlets of wretched round huts with conical roofs, peopled by a very poor apparently harmless set, whose wants appear almost as small as their possessions. The greater part are without waist cloths, and the only ornaments I observed were pieces of wood in the ears. They have a few fouls and one or two goats were brought for sale. They raise Millo, Cassava and rice, collect a little honey, catch a few mud fish from the Lake and shoot occasionally an antelope, but they have no cattle which Dr. Livingstone accounted for by observing the Tetsee, a species of fly which he had found by long experience to be entirely destructive to every kind of domestic cattle except the ass. On the western slope of the hill were [a] large number of Ebony trees. I regretted much not having time to spend to cut and take one down to the ship. On the surface we saw a good deal of lignite from which Dr. Livingstone inferred the vicinity of coal. There were many traces of antelopes and other wild animals but we saw none of them, though the natives brought us some small skins. Many of the trees, plants and bushes were entirely new and very interesting though difficult to describe. One plant bore a most beautiful scarlet and yellow flower which would have been highly prized in an English conservatory and is I fancy new to us—some of the seed vessels were very remarkable, one which they called the cow itch was dangerous to touch.

After our walk Dr. Livingstone, Mr. Playfair and I had our last dinner together under my tent. I had taken my cook and he served us capitally, in fact we had every meal as comfortably as I should have had on board the Orestes.

We had much talk after dinner over Dr. Livingstone's future plans and movements. His object in ascending the Rovuma is to find a water communication to Lake Nyassa or at any rate to a spot within an easy journey of it—he has been informed by the natives that the Rovuma runs out of the Nyassa, but it seems hardly possible if it is true that that Lake is 1200 feet above the sea, that the river can be navigable. Judging from the dimensions up to the point we ascended it and the force of its current it is not probable that there is any great rise in its bed—and if its source is from the Nyassa or on a level with it, there must be a great number of cataracts in its upper part.

We very much doubted whether Dr. Livingstone would succeed in getting up much farther, but it may be that we are still only in the delta of the river and that when the several branches of its mouth form into one stream, it may possess more volume.

During the last few days I had seen a great deal of Dr. Livingstone and got to like him very much. He is modest, gentle and quiet and utterly fearless, and thus inspires confidence among the native tribes with which he is thrown in contact—his brother seems a good kind man but without the Doctor's ability. Dr. Kirk who is the medical man and naturalist of the expedition is a fine active man of about thirty, very able and intelligent, he has been suffering from fever during the last few days, and will probably have to go to Europe for a change. Mr. Rae the Engineer had dysentery at the time of leaving the ship and was obliged to go back with us to the Pioneer. Mr. Rae came out with a small steamer to go on Lake Nyassa. They have succeeded in getting it up to the head of the Shire but there remains a land transport which I doubt much if they will ever succeed in effecting. She takes to pieces but some of the parts weigh 5 or 6 tons.

Sept 11th

Parted from Dr. Livingstone's party on our descent at 6 A.M. Gave them three cheers.

Our course down the river was more rapid than the ascent but there were many places which we had a difficulty in getting the cutter over, and we thought the river had fallen since we went up. We had many tempting shots at birds. There were immense flocks of a large black goose which weigh 12 lbs each but we could not succeed in getting any. There were also numerous other large birds that were quite strangers to us: a large vulture, a fish eagle of a beautiful chocolate colour, razor bills, spoon bills, strange looking chicks, all kinds of herons, cranes, &c., ibises, the Egyptian brown geese, horn bills, kingfishers, the fishing eagle pigeons and goat suckers. An immense number of hippopotami; we saw traces of buffaloes, koodoos, steinboks and water buck, and we thought we saw a crocodile but these are rare, and there does not seem to be any great plenty of fish in this river.

We reached the mouth of the river at Sunset, having left the cutter far astern after making sail.

.   .   .   .   .

[September] 24th

[Off Mogadishu] Eight of our party up the Rovuma reported on the sick list with fever. . . . I pray to God to deal mercifully with us.

.   .   .   .   .

1863

[January] 23rd [Simon's Bay] . . . I received a letter from Dr. Livingstone dated 15th October Rovuma and with a postscript of about the 24th from Pomony when he had met the Gorgon.

He tells me that after parting with us at the *Lakelet*

Chidia the river improved a little, with hills on each side from 500 to 600 feet high, upon ascending one of which they proved to be the edge of a densely wooded table land with a good deal of cultivation on it. 60 miles up he came to people living on sand banks for fear of being stolen, who in turn lost no chance of stealing others. Above this they were shot at with arrows by a party of natives from a high bank and notwithstanding Dr. Livingstone's expostulation and presents this was repeated, when a well directed volley from the boats sent them all but scampering. After this they seem to have met no unfriendly treatment. Higher up the river there was a good deal of canoe traffic with rice and salt.

The Highlands were found to extend about 80 miles (probably from the mouth). They then retire and leave an extended plain with (?) and thin granitic hills.

The party ascended 114 miles in a straight line though 156 following the curves of the river. They turned at a small cataract Latd. 11. 13 s. Long. 38°. 39' E. Before turning the river had become choked with large rocks through which canoes passed but the boats could not. The expedition were on the slave trade route from Nyassa to Quiloa. About 40 miles above the point they reached the Rovuma is joined by the river *Liende* or *Niende*, which has its source in the mountains East of Lake Nyassa. The confluence of the Liende with the Rovuma is called Ngomano.

The natives still continue to say that the Rovuma comes out of Lake Nyassa.

EDITORIAL NOTE

The drawing facing, and the tailpiece on page 204, are based on the original plate in ZT, *p.* 439. *They show the method of catching fish on the Rovuma, described on p.* 76 *above, and (tailpiece) a beehive. The beehive is of a type similar to that described by James Bruce in his travels.*

EXTRACT FROM DAVID AND
CHARLES LIVINGSTONE'S

Narrative of an Expedition
to the Zambesi and its Tributaries

LONDON, 1865

THIS EXTRACT (from pages 427-455 of Livingstone's 1865 book on the Zambezi Expedition) covers the period of the Rovuma field notebook for 23 August 1862 to 19 March 1863.

By the time everything had been placed on board the Lady Nyassa, the waters of the Zambesi and the Shire had fallen so low that it was useless to attempt taking her up to the cataracts before the rains in December. Draught oxen and provisions also were required, and could not be obtained nearer than the Island of Johanna. The Portuguese, without refusing positively to let trade enter the Zambesi, threw impediments in the way; they only wanted a small duty! They were about to establish a river police, and rearrange the Crown lands, which have long since become Zulu lands; meanwhile they were making the Zambesi, by slaving, of no value to any one.

The Rovuma, which was reported to come from Lake Nyassa, being out of the claims and a free river, we determined to explore it in our boats immediately on our return from Johanna, for which place after some delay at the Kongone, in repairing engines, paddle-wheel, and rudder, we sailed on the 6th of August. A store of naval provisions had been formed on a hulk in Pomone Bay of that island for the supply of the cruisers, and was in charge of Mr. Sunley, the Consul, from whom we always received the kindest attentions and assistance. He now obliged us by parting with six oxen, trained for his own use in sugar-making. Though sadly hampered in his undertaking by being obliged to employ slave labour, he has by indomitable energy overcome obstacles under which most persons would have sunk. He has done all that under the circumstances could be done to infuse a desire for freedom, by paying regular wages; and has established a large factory, and brought 300 acres of rich soil under cultivation with sugar-cane. We trust he will realize the fortune, which he so well deserves to earn. Had Mr Sunley performed the same experiment on the mainland, where people would have flocked to him for the wages he now gives, he would certainly have inaugurated a new era on the East Coast of Africa. On a small island where the slaveholders have complete power over the slaves, and where there is no free soil such as is everywhere met with in Africa, the experiment ought not to be repeated. Were Mr Sunley commencing again, it should neither be in Zanzibar nor Johanna, but on African soil, where, if even a slave is ill-treated, he can easily by flight become free. On an island under native rule a joint manufacture by Arabs and Englishmen might only mean that the latter were to escape the odium of flogging the slaves.

On leaving Johanna and our oxen for a time, H.M.S. Orestes towed us thence to the mouth of the Rovuma at the beginning of September. Captain Gardner her commander, and several of his officers, accompanied us up the river for two days in the gig and cutter. The water was unusually low, and it was rather dull work for a few hours in the morning; but the scene became livelier and more animated when the breeze began to blow. Our four boats then swept on under full sail, the men on the look-out in the gig and cutter calling, "Port, sir!" "Starboard, sir!" "As you go, sir!" while the black men in the bows of the others shouted the practical equivalents, "Pagombe! Pagombe!" "Enda quete!" "Berane! Berane!" Presently the leading-boat touches on a sandbank; down comes the fluttering sail; the men jump out to shove her off, and the other boats, shunning the obstruction, shoot on ahead to be brought up each in its turn by mistaking a sandbank for the channel, which had often but a very little depth of water.

A drowsy herd of hippopotami were suddenly startled by a score of rifle-shots, and stared in amazement at the strange objects which had invaded their peaceful domains, until a few more bullets compelled them to seek refuge at the bottom of the deep pool, near which they had been quietly reposing. On our return, one of the herd retaliated. He followed the boat, came up under it, and twice tried to tear the bottom out of it; but fortunately it was too flat for his jaws to get a good gripe, so he merely damaged one of the planks with his tusks, though he lifted the boat right up, with ten men and a ton of ebony in it.

We slept, one of the two nights Captain Gardner was with us, opposite the lakelet Chidia, which is connected with the river in flood time, and is nearly surrounded by hills some 500 or 600 feet high, dotted over with trees. A few small groups of huts stood on the hill-sides, with gardens off which the usual native produce had been reaped. The people did not seem much alarmed by the presence of the large party which had drawn up on the sandbanks below their dwellings. There is abundance of large ebony in the neighbourhood. The pretty little antelope (*Cephalophus cœruleus*), about the size of a hare, seemed to abound, as many of their skins were offered for sale. Neat figured date-leaf mats of various colours are woven here, the different dyes being obtained from the barks of trees. Cattle could not live on the banks of the Rovuma on account of the tsetse, which are found from near the mouth, up as far as we could take the boats. The navigation did not improve as we ascended; snags, brought down by the floods, were common, and left in the channel on the sudden subsidence of the water. In many places, where the river divided into two or three channels, there was not water enough in any of them for a boat drawing three feet, so we had to drag ours over the shoals; but we saw the river at its very lowest, and it may be years before it is so dried up again.

The valley of the Rovuma, bounded on each side by a range of highlands, is from two to four miles in width, and comes in a pretty straight course from the W.S.W.; but the channel of the river is winding, and now at its lowest zigzagged so perversely, that frequently the boats had to pass over three miles to make one in a straight line. With a full stream it must of course be much easier work. Few natives were seen during the first week. Their villages are concealed in the thick jungle on the hill-sides, for protection from marauding slave-parties. Not much of interest was observed on this part of the silent and shallow river. Though feeling convinced that it was unfit for navigation, except for eight months of the year, we pushed on, resolved to see if, further inland, the accounts we had received from different naval officers of its great capabilities would prove correct; or if, by communication with Lake Nyassa, even the upper part could be turned to account. Our exploration showed us, that the greatest precaution is required in those who visit new countries.

The reports we received from gentlemen, who had entered the river and were well qualified to judge, were that the Rovuma was infinitely superior to the Zambesi, in the absence of any bar at its mouth, in its greater volume of water, and in the beauty of the adjacent lands. We probably came at a different season from that in which they visited it, and our account ought to be taken with theirs to arrive at the truth. It might be available as a highway for commerce during three quarters of each year; but casual visitors, like ourselves and others, are ill able to decide. The absence of bird or animal life was remarkable. Occasionally we saw pairs of the stately jabirus, or adjutant-looking marabouts, wading among the shoals, and spurwinged geese, and other water-fowl, but there was scarcely a crocodile or a hippopotamus to be seen.

At the end of the first week, an old man called at our camp, and said he would send a present from his village, which was up among the hills. He appeared next morning with a number of his people, bringing meal, cassava-root, and yams. The language differs considerably from that on the Zambesi, but it is of the same family. The people are Makonde, and are on friendly terms with the Mabiha, and the Makoa, who live south of the Rovuma. When taking a walk up the slopes of the north bank, we found a great variety of trees we had seen nowhere else. Those usually met with far inland seem here to approach the coast. African ebony, generally named *mpingu*, is abundant within eight miles of the sea; it attains a larger size, and has more of the interior black wood than usual. A good timber tree called *mosoko* is also found; and we saw half-caste Arabs near the coast cutting up a large log of it into planks. Before reaching the top of the rise we were in a forest of bamboos. On the plateau above, large patches were cleared and cultivated. A man invited us to take a cup of beer; on our complying with his request, the fear previously shown by the bystanders vanished. Our Mazaro men could hardly understand what they said. Some of them waded in the river and caught a curious fish in holes in the claybank. Its ventral fin is peculiar, being unusually large, and of a circular shape, like boys' playthings called 'suckers'. We were told that this fish is found also in the Zambesi, and is called Chirire. Though all its fins are large, it is asserted that it rarely ventures out into the stream, but remains near its hole, where it is readily caught by the hand.

The Zambesi men thoroughly understood the characteristic marks of deep or shallow water, and showed great skill in finding out the proper channel. The Molimo is the steersman at the helm, the Mokadamo is the head canoe-man, and he stands erect on the bows with a long pole in his hands, and directs the steersman where to go, aiding the rudder, if necessary, with his pole. The others preferred to stand and punt our boat, rather than row with our long oars, being able to shove her ahead faster than they could pull her. They are accustomed to short paddles. Our Mokadamo was affected with moon-blindness, and could not see at all at night. His comrades then led him about, and handed him his food. They thought that it was only because his eyes rested all night, that he could see the channel so well by day. At difficult places the Mokadamo sometimes, however, made mistakes, and ran us aground; and the others, evidently imbued with the spirit of resistance to constituted authority, and led by Joao an aspirant for the office, jeered him for his stupidity. "Was he asleep? Why did he allow the boat to come there? Could he not see the channel was somewhere else?" At last the Mokadamo threw down the pole in disgust, and told Joao he might be a Mokadamo himself. The office was accepted with alacrity; but in a few minutes he too ran us into a worse difficulty than his predecessor ever did, and was at once disrated amidst the derision of his comrades.

In travelling it is best to enjoy the little simple incidents of this kind, which, at most, exemplify the tendencies woven into the being of the whole human family. It is a pity to hear that some of our countrymen rudely interfere in what really does no harm. Blows even have been inflicted under the silly assumption that the negro is this, that, and the other thing, and not, like other men, a curious mixture of good and evil, wisdom and folly, cleverness and stupidity. An Englishman possessed of a gun, which had the ugly trick of going off of itself, came up the Zambesi in a canoe manned by natives. He scarcely knew another word of the language than the verb "*to kill*". The gun, as was its wont, accidentally went off close to the head of one of the party, who, before going to sleep, expressed his fears to his comrades that this unlucky gun might "*kill*" some of them. Our hero caught the word, and spent the whole night revolver in hand, ready to punish the treachery which existed only in his own excited brain. This adventure he afterwards published in a newspaper as a terrible situation, a hairbreadth escape from bloodthirsty savages. Another British Lion, having to travel some two hundred miles in a canoe, and being unable to speak a word of the language, thought it clever to fire off all the barrels of his revolver every time his canoe-men proposed to land during the live-long day. The torrid sun right overhead was at its hottest. The poor fellows made signs they wished to purchase some beer. Off went the revolver, "No, no, no, paddle you must." This madness, as described to us by himself, was evidently thought clever. Another, whose estimate of himself and that formed of him by a tribe he visited did not at all coincide, after complaining at a public meeting of the untruthfulness of a previous traveller to whom that same tribe had shown distinguished kindness and respect, stated, as we learn on the authority of a clergyman who was present, that he had tied up one of his people before reaching the tribe referred to, "and given him a sound thrashing". Let us fancy the effect on an English village if a black man came to it, and a white servant complained that he had been maltreated by him on the way. We have felt heartily ashamed sometimes on discovering how causelessly we have been angry. No doubt the natives are at times as perversely stupid as servants at home can be when they like; but our conduct must often appear to the native mind as a mixture of silliness and insanity.

On the 16th September, we arrived at the inhabited island of Kichokomane. The usual way of approaching an unknown people is to call out in a cheerful tone "Malonda!" Things for sale, or do you want to sell anything? If we can obtain a man from the last village, he is employed, though only useful in explaining to the next that we come in a friendly way. The people here were shy of us at first, and could not be induced to sell any food; until a woman, more adventurous than the rest, sold us a fowl. This opened the market, and crowds came with fowls and meal, far beyond our wants. The women are as ugly as those on Lake Nyassa, for who can be handsome wearing the pelele or upper-lip ring of large dimensions? We were once surprised to see young men wearing the pelele, and were told that in the tribe of the Mabiha, on the south bank, men as well as women wore them.

Along the left bank, above Kichokomane, is an exceedingly fertile plain, nearly two miles broad, and studded with a number of deserted villages. The inhabitants were living in temporary huts on low naked sandbanks; and we found this to be the case as far as we went. They leave most of their property and food behind, because they are not afraid of these being stolen, but only fear being stolen themselves. The great slave-route from Nyassa to Kilwa passes to N.E. from S.W., just beyond them; and it is dangerous to remain in their villages at this time of year, when the kidnappers are abroad. In one of the temporary villages, we saw, in passing, two human heads lying on the ground. We slept a couple of miles above this village.

Before sunrise next morning, a large party armed with bows and arrows and muskets came to the camp, two or three of them having a fowl each, which we refused to purchase, having bought enough the day before. They followed us all the morning, and after breakfast those on the left bank swam across and joined the main party on the other side. It was evidently their intention to attack us at a chosen spot, where we had to pass close to a high bank, but their plan was frustrated by a stiff breeze sweeping the boats past, before the majority could get to the place. They disappeared then, but came out again ahead of us, on a high wooded bank, walking rapidly to the bend, near which we were obliged to sail. An arrow was shot at the foremost boat; and seeing the force at the bend, we pushed out from the side, as far as the shoal water would permit, and tried to bring them to a parley, by declaring, that we had not come to fight, but to see the river. "Why did you fire a gun, a little while ago?" they asked. "We shot a large puff-adder, to prevent it from killing men; you may see it lying dead on the beach." With great courage, our Mokadamo waded to within thirty yards of the bank, and spoke with much earnestness, assuring them that we were a peaceable party, and had not come for war, but to see the river. We were friends, and our countrymen bought cotton and ivory, and wished to come and trade with them. All we wanted was to go up quietly to look at the river, and then return to the sea again. While he was talking with those on the shore, the old rogue, who appeared to be the ringleader, stole up the bank, and with a dozen others, waded across to the island, near which the boats lay, and came down behind us. Wild with excitement, they rushed into the water, and danced in our rear, with drawn bows, taking aim, and making various savage gesticulations. Their leader urged them to get behind some snags, and then shoot at us. The party on the bank in front had many muskets—and those of them, who had bows, held them with arrows ready set in the bowstrings. They had a mass of thick bush and trees behind them, into which they could in a moment dart, after discharging their muskets and arrows, and be completely hidden from our sight; a circumstance that always gives people who use bows and arrows the greatest confidence. Notwithstanding these demonstrations, we were exceedingly loath to come to blows. We spent a full half-hour exposed at any moment to be struck by a bullet or poisoned arrow. We explained that we were better armed than they were, and had plenty of ammunition, the suspected want of which often inspires them with courage, but that we did not wish to shed the blood of the children of the same Great Father with ourselves; that if we must fight, the guilt would be all theirs.

This being a common mode of expostulation among themselves, we so far succeeded, that with great persuasion the leader and others laid down their arms, and waded over from the bank to the boats to talk the matter over. "This was their river; they did not allow white men to use it. We must pay toll for leave to pass." It was somewhat humiliating to do so, but it was pay or fight; and, rather than fight, we submitted to the humiliation of paying for their friendship, and gave them thirty yards of cloth. They pledged themselves to be our friends ever afterwards, and said they would have food cooked for us on our return. We then hoisted sail, and proceeded, glad that the affair had been amicably settled. Those on shore walked up to the bend above to look at the boat, as we supposed; but, the moment she was abreast of them, they gave us a volley of musket-balls and poisoned arrows, without a word of warning. Fortunately we were so near, that all the arrows passed clear over us, but four musket-balls went through the sail just above our heads. All our assailants bolted into the bushes and long grass, the instant after firing, save two, one of whom was about to discharge a musket and the other an arrow, when arrested by the fire of the second boat. Not one of them showed their faces again, till we were a thousand yards away. A few shots were then fired over their heads, to give them an idea of the range of our rifles, and they all fled into the woods. Those on the sandbank rushed off too, with the utmost speed; but, as they had not shot at us, we did not molest them, and they went off safely with their cloth. They probably expected to kill one of our number, and in the confusion rob the boats. It is only where the people are slavers, that the natives of this part of Africa are bloodthirsty.

These people have a bad name in the country in front, even among their own tribe. A slave-trading Arab we met above, thinking we were then on our way down the river, advised us not to land at the villages, but to stay in the boats, as the inhabitants were treacherous, and attacked at once, without any warning or provocation. Our experience of their conduct fully confirmed the truth of what he said. There was no trade on the river where they lived, but beyond that part there was a brisk canoe-trade in rice and salt; those further in the interior cultivating rice, and sending it down the river to be exchanged for salt, which is extracted from the earth in certain places on the banks. Our assailants hardly anticipated resistance, and told a neighbouring Chief, that if they had known who we were, they would not have attacked English, who can "bite hard". They offered no molestations on our way down, though we were an hour in passing their village. Our canoe-men plucked up courage on finding that we had come off unhurt. One of them named Chiku, acknowledging that he had been terribly frightened, said "His fear was not the kind which makes a man jump overboard and run away; but that which brings the heart up to the mouth, and renders the man powerless, and no more able to fight than a woman."

In the country of Chonga Michi, about 80 or 90 miles up the river, we found decent people, though of the same tribe, who treated strangers with civility. A body of Makoa had come from their own country in the south, and settled here. The Makoa are known by a cicatrice in the forehead shaped like the new moon with the horns turned downwards. The tribe possesses all the country

189

west of Mosambique; and they will not allow any of the Portuguese to pass into their country more than two hours' distance from the fort. A hill some ten or twelve miles distant, called Pau, has been visited during the present generation only by one Portuguese and one English officer, and this visit was accomplished only by the influence of the private friendship of a Chief for this Portuguese gentleman. Our allies have occupied the Fort of Mosambique for three hundred years, but in this, as in all other cases, have no power further than they can see from a gun-carriage.

The Makoa chief, Matingula, was hospitable and communicative, telling us all he knew of the river and country beyond. He had been once to Iboe and once at Mosambique with slaves. Our men understood his language easily. A useless musket he had bought at one of the above places was offered us for a little cloth. Having received a present of food from him, a railway rug was handed to him: he looked at it—had never seen cloth like that before—did not approve of it, and would rather have cotton cloth. "But this will keep you warm at night."—"Oh I do not wish to be kept warm at night."—We gave him a bit of cotton cloth, not one-third the value of the rug, but it was more highly prized. His people refused to sell their fowls for our splendid prints and drab cloths. They had probably been taken in with gaudy-patterned sham prints before. They preferred a very cheap, plain, blue stuff of which they had experience. A great quantity of excellent honey is collected all along the river, by bark hives being placed for the bees on the high trees on both banks. Large pots of it, very good and clear, were offered in exchange for a very little cloth. No wax was brought for sale; there being no market for this commodity it is probably thrown away as useless.

At Michi we lose the table-land which, up to this point, bounds the view on both sides of the river, as it were, with ranges of flat-topped hills, 600 or 800 feet high; and to this plateau a level fertile plain succeeds, on which stand detached granite hills. That portion of the table-land on the right bank seems to bend away to the south, still preserving the appearance of a hill range. The height opposite extends a few miles further west, and then branches off in a northerly direction. A few small pieces of coal were picked up on the sandbanks, showing that this useful mineral exists on the Rovuma, or on some of its tributaries: the natives know that it will burn. At the lakelet Chidia, we noticed the same sandstone rock, with fossil wood on it, which we have on the Zambesi, and knew to be a sure evidence of coal beneath. We mentioned this at the time to Captain Gardner, and our finding coal now seemed a verification of what we then said; the coalfield probably extends from the Zambesi to the Rovuma, if not beyond it. Some of the rocks lower down have the permanent water-line three feet above the present height of the water.

A few miles west of the Makoa of Matingula, we came again among the Makonde, but now of good repute. War and slavery have driven them to seek refuge on the sandbanks. A venerable-looking old man hailed us as we passed, and asked us if we were going by without speaking. We landed, and he laid down his gun and came to us; he was accompanied by his brother, who shook hands with every one in the boat, as he had seen people do at Kilwa. "Then you have seen white men before?" we said. "Yes," replied the polite African, "but never people of your quality." These men were very black, and wore but little clothing. A young woman, dressed in the highest style of Makonde fashion, punting as dexterously as a man could, brought a canoe full of girls to see us. She wore an ornamental head-dress of red beads tied to her hair on one side of her head, a necklace of fine beads of various colours, two bright figured brass bracelets on her left arm, and scarcely a farthing's worth of cloth, though it was at its cheapest.

As we pushed on westwards, we found that the river makes a little southing, and some reaches were deeper than any near the sea; but when we had ascended about 140 miles by the river's course from the sea, soft tufa rocks began to appear; ten miles beyond, the river became more narrow and rocky, and when, according to our measurement, we had ascended 156 miles, our further progress was arrested. We were rather less than two degrees in a straight line from the Coast. The incidents worth noticing were but few: seven canoes with loads of salt and rice kept company with us for some days, and the further we went inland, the more civil the people became.

When we came to a stand, just below the island of Nyamatolo, Long. 38° 36′ E., and Lat. 11° 53′, the river was narrow, and full of rocks. Near the island there is a rocky rapid with narrow passages fit only for native canoes; the fall is small, and the banks quite low; but these rocks were an effectual barrier to all further progress in boats. Previous reports represented the navigable part of this river as extending to the distance of a month's sail from its mouth; we found that, at the ordinary heights of the water, a boat might reach the obstructions which seem peculiar to all African rivers in six or eight days. The Rovuma is remarkable for the high lands that flank it for some eighty miles from the ocean. The cataracts of other rivers occur in mountains, those of the Rovuma are found in a level part, with hills only in the distance. Far away in the west and north we could see high blue heights, probably of igneous origin from their forms, rising out of a plain.

The distance from Ngomano, a spot thirty miles further up, to the Arab crossing-places of Lake Nyassa Tsenga or Kotakota was said to be twelve days. The way we had discovered to Lake Nyassa by Murchison's Cataracts had so much less land carriage, that we considered it best to take our steamer thither, by the route in which we were well known, instead of working where we were strangers; and accordingly we made up our minds to return.

The natives reported a worse place above our turning-point—the passage being still narrower than this. An Arab, they said, once built a boat above the rapids, and sent it down full of slaves; but it was broken to pieces in these upper narrows. Many still maintained that the Rovuma came from Nyassa, and that it is very narrow as it issues out of the lake. One man declared that he had seen it with his own eyes as it left the lake, and seemed displeased at being cross-questioned, as if we doubted his veracity.

More satisfactory information, as it appeared to us, was obtained from others. Two days, or thirty miles, beyond where we turned back, the Rovuma is joined by the Liende, which, coming from the south-west, rises in the mountains on the east side of Nyassa. The great slave route to Kilwa runs up the banks of this river, which is only ankle-deep at the dry season of the year. The Rovuma itself comes from the W.N.W., and after the traveller passes the confluence of the Liende at Ngomano or "meeting-place", the Chief of which part is named Ndonde, he finds the river narrow, and the people Ajawa.

The Nyamatolo people have a great abundance of food, and they cultivate the land extensively. The island is simply their summer residence; their permanent villages being in the woods. While hunting, we entered some of these villages, and saw that large quantities of grain were left in them, and in some parts of the forest away from the villages we found many pots of oil-yielding seeds (sesamum), besides grain. The sesamum was offered to us both for sale and as a present, under the name *mafuta*, or fat; and small quantities of gum copal were also brought to us, which led us to think that these articles may have been collected by the Arabs. Tobacco, formed into lumps, was abundant and cheap. Cotton-bushes were seen, but no one was observed spinning or weaving cotton for anything but fishing-nets. The article of most value was a climbing dye-wood, which attains the thickness of a man's leg, and which Dr Kirk has found experimentally to be of considerable value as a fast yellow colour. Baobab-trees on the Rovuma, though not nearly so gigantic in size as those on the Zambesi, bear fruit more than twice as large. The great white blossoms were just out, and much of last year's fruit was still hanging on the branches.

Crocodiles in the Rovuma have a sorry time of it. Never before were reptiles so persecuted and snubbed. They are hunted with spears, and spring traps are set for them. If one of them enters an inviting pool after fish, he soon finds a fence thrown round it, and a spring trap set in the only path out of the enclosure. Their flesh is eaten, and relished. The banks, on which the female lays her eggs by night, are carefully searched by day, and all the eggs dug out and devoured. The fish-hawk makes havoc among the few young ones that escape their other enemies. Our men were constantly on the look-out for crocodiles' nests. One was found containing thirty-five newly-laid eggs, and they declared that the crocodile would lay as many more the second night in another place. The eggs were a foot deep in the sand on the top of a bank ten feet high. The animal digs a hole with its foot, covers the eggs, and leaves them till the river rises over the nest in about three months afterwards, when she comes back, and assists the young ones out. We once saw opposite Tette young crocodiles in December, swimming beside an island in company with an old one. The yolk of the egg is nearly as white as the real white. In taste they resemble hen's eggs with perhaps a smack of custard, and would be as highly relished by whites as by blacks, were it not for their unsavoury origin in men-eaters.

Hunting the Senze (*Aulacodus Swindernianus*), an animal the size of a large cat, but in shape more like a pig, was the chief business of men and boys as we passed the reedy banks and low islands. They set fire to a mass of reeds, and, armed with sticks, spears, bows and arrows, stand in groups guarding the outlets through which the scared Senze may run from the approaching flames. Dark dense volumes of impenetrable smoke now roll over on the lee side of the islet, and shroud the hunters. At times vast sheets of lurid flames bursting forth, roaring, crackling and exploding, leap wildly far above the tall reeds. Out rush the terrified animals, and amid the smoke are

194

seen the excited hunters dancing about with frantic gesticulations, and hurling stick, spear, and arrow at their burned out victims. Kites hover over the smoke, ready to pounce on the mantis and locusts as they spring from the fire. Small crows and hundreds of swallows are on eager wing, darting into the smoke and out again, seizing fugitive flies. Scores of insects, in their haste to escape from the fire, jump into the river, and the active fish enjoy a rare feast.

We returned to the Pioneer on the 9th of October, having been away one month. The ship's company had used distilled water, a condenser having been sent out from England; and there had not been a single case of sickness on board since we left, though there were so many cases of fever the few days she lay in the same spot last year. Our boat party drank the water of the river, and the three white sailors, who had never been in an African river before, had some slight attacks of fever.

.   .   .   .   .

We put to sea on the 18th of October, and, again touching at Johanna, obtained a crew of Johanna men and some oxen, and sailed for the Zambesi; but our fuel failing before we reached it, and the wind being contrary, we ran into Quillimane for wood.

Quillimane must have been built solely for the sake of carrying on the slave-trade, for no man in his senses would ever have dreamed of placing a village on such a low, muddy, fever-haunted, and mosquito-swarming site, had it not been for the facilities it afforded for slaving. The bar may at springs and floods be easily crossed by sailing-vessels, but, being far from the land, it is always dangerous for boats. Slaves, under the name of "free emigrants", have gone by thousands from Quillimane, during the last six years, to the ports a little to the south, particularly to Massangano. Some excellent brick-houses still stand in the place, and the owners are generous and hospitable: among them our good friend, Colonel Nuñez. His disinterested kindness to us and to all our countrymen can never be forgotten. He is a noble example of what energy and uprightness may accomplish even here. He came out as a cabin-boy, and, without a single friend to help him, he has persevered in an honourable course until he is the richest man on the East Coast. When Dr Livingstone came down the Zambesi in 1856, Colonel Nuñez was the chief of the only four honourable, trustworthy men in the country. But while he has risen, a whole herd has sunk, making loud lamentations, through puffs of cigar-smoke, over negro laziness; they might add, their own.

All agricultural enterprise is virtually discouraged by the Quillimane Government. A man must purchase a permit from the Governor, when he wishes to visit his country farm; and this tax, in a country where labour is unpopular, causes the farms to be almost entirely left in the hands of a head slave, who makes returns to his master as interest or honesty prompts him. A passport must also be bought whenever a man wishes to go up the river to Mazaro, Senna, or Tette, or even to reside for a month at Quillimane. With a soil and a climate well suited for the growth of the cane, abundance of slave labour, and water communication to any market in the world, they have never made their own sugar. All they use is imported from Bombay. "The people of Quillimane have no enterprise," said a young European Portuguese, "they do nothing, and are always wasting their time in suffering, or in recovering from fever."

We entered the Zambesi about the end of November and found it unusually low, so we did not get up to Shupanga till the 19th of December. The friends of our Mazaro men, who had now become good sailors and very attentive servants, turned out and gave them a hearty welcome back from the perils of the sea: they had begun to fear that they would never return. We hired them at a sixteen-yard piece of cloth a month—about ten shillings' worth, the Portuguese market-price of the cloth being then sevenpence halfpenny a yard,—and paid them five pieces each, for four-and-a-half months' work. A merchant at the same time paid other Mazaro men three pieces for seven months, and they were with him in the interior. If the merchants do not prosper, it is not because labour is dear, but because it is scarce, and because they are so eager on every occasion to sell the workmen out of the country. Our men had also received quantities of good clothes from the sailors of the Pioneer and of the Orestes, and were now regarded by their neighbours and by themselves as men of importance. Never before had they possessed so much wealth: they believed that they might settle in life, being now of sufficient standing to warrant their entering the married state; and a wife and a hut were among their first investments. Sixteen yards were paid to the wife's parents, and a hut cost four yards. We should have liked to have kept them in the ship, for they were well-behaved and had learned a great deal of the work required. Though they would not themselves go again, they engaged others for us; and brought twice as many as we could take, of their brothers and cousins, who were eager to join the ship and go with us up the Shire, or anywhere else. They all agreed to take half-pay until they too had learned to work; and we found no scarcity of labour, though all that could be exported is now out of the country.

There had been a drought of unusual severity during the past season in the country between Lupata and Kebrabasa, and it had extended north-east to the Manganja highlands. All the Tette slaves, except a very few household ones, had been driven away by hunger, and were now far off in the woods, and wherever wild fruit, or the prospect of obtaining anything whatever to keep the breath of life in them, was to be found. Their masters were said never to expect to see them again. There have been two years of great hunger at Tette since we have been in the country, and a famine like the present prevailed in 1854, when thousands died of starvation. If men like the Cape farmers owned this country, their energy and enterprise would soon render the crops independent of rain. There being plenty of slope or fall, the land could be easily irrigated from the Zambesi and its tributary streams. A Portuguese colony can never prosper: it is used as a penal settlement, and everything must be done military fashion. "What do I care for this country?" said the most enterprising of the Tette merchants, "all I want is to make money as soon as possible, and then go to Bombay and enjoy it." All business at Tette was now suspended. Carriers could not be found to take the goods into the interior, and the merchants could barely obtain food for their own families. At Mazaro more rain had fallen, and a tolerable crop followed. The people of Shupanga were collecting and drying different wild fruits, nearly all of which are far from palatable to a European taste. The root of a small creeper called "bisé" is dug up and eaten. In appearance it is not unlike the small white sweet potato, and has a little of the flavour of our potato. It would be very good, if it were only a little larger. From another tuber, called "ulanga", very good starch can be made. A few miles from Shupanga there is an abundance of large game, but the people here, though fond enough of meat, are not a hunting race, and seldom kill any.

The Shire having risen, we steamed off on the 10th of January, 1863, with the Lady Nyassa in tow. It was not long before we came upon the ravages of the notorious Mariano. The survivors of a small hamlet, at the foot of Morambala, were in a state of starvation, having lost their food by one of his marauding parties. The women were in the fields collecting insects, roots, wild fruits, and whatever could be eaten, in order to drag on their lives, if possible, till the next crop should be ripe. Two canoes passed us, that had been robbed by Mariano's band of everything they had in them; the owners were gathering palm-nuts for their subsistence. They wore palm-leaf aprons, as the robbers had stripped them of their clothing and ornaments. Dead bodies floated past us daily, and in the mornings the paddles had to be cleared of corpses, caught by the floats during the night. For scores of miles the entire population of the valley was swept away by this scourge Mariano, who is again, as he was before, the great Portuguese slave-agent. It made the heart ache to see the wide-spread desolation; the river-banks, once so populous, all silent; the villages burned down, and an oppressive stillness reigning where formerly crowds of eager sellers appeared with the various products of their industry. Here and there might be seen on the bank a small dreary deserted shed, where had sat, day after day, a starving fisherman, until the rising waters drove the fish from their wonted haunts, and left him to die. Tingane had been defeated; his people had been killed, kidnapped, and forced to flee from their villages. There were a few wretched survivors in a village above the Ruo; but the majority of the population was dead. The sight and smell of dead bodies was everywhere. Many skeletons lay beside the path, where in their weakness they had fallen and expired. Ghastly living forms of boys and girls, with dull dead eyes, were crouching beside some of the huts. A few more miserable days of their terrible hunger, and they would be with the dead.

Oppressed with the shocking scenes around, we visited the Bishop's grave; and though it matters little where a good Christian's ashes rest, yet it was with sadness that we thought over the hopes which had clustered around him, as he left the classic grounds of Cambridge, all now buried in this wild place. How it would have torn his kindly heart to witness the sights we now were forced to see!

In giving vent to the natural feelings of regret, that a man so eminently endowed and learned, as was Bishop Mackenzie, should have been so soon cut off, some have expressed an opinion that it was wrong to use an instrument so valuable *merely* to convert the heathen. If the attempt is to be made at all, it is "penny wise and pound foolish" to employ any but the very best men, and those who are specially educated for the work. An ordinary clergyman, however well suited for a parish, will not, without special training, make a Missionary; and as to their comparative usefulness, it is like that of the man who builds an hospital, as compared with that of the surgeon who in after years only administers for a time the remedies which the founder had provided in perpetuity. Had the Bishop succeeded in introducing Christianity, his converts might have been few, but they would have formed a continuous roll for all time to come.

The Shire fell two feet, before we reached the shallow crossing where we had formerly such difficulty, and we had now two ships to take up. A hippopotamus was shot two miles above a bank on which the ship lay a fortnight: it floated in three hours. As the boat was towing it down, the crocodiles were attracted by the dead beast, and several shots had to be fired to keep them off. The bullet had not entered the brain of the animal, but driven a splinter of bone into it. A little moisture with some gas issued from the wound, and this was all that could tell the crocodiles down the stream of a dead hippopotamus; and yet they came up from miles below. Their sense of smell must be as acute as their hearing; both are quite extraordinary. Dozens fed on the meat we left. Our Krooman, Jumbo, used to assert, that the crocodile never eats fresh meat, but always keeps it till it is high and tender—and the stronger it smells, the better he likes it. There seems to be some truth in this. They can swallow but small pieces at a time, and find it difficult to tear fresh meat. In the act of swallowing, which is like that of a dog, the head is raised out of the water. We tried to catch some, and one was soon hooked; it required half-a-dozen hands to haul him up the river, and the shark-hook straightened, and he got away. A large iron hook was next made, but, as the creatures could not swallow it, their jaws soon pressed it straight—and our crocodile-fishing was a failure. As one might expect,—from the power even of a salmon—the tug of a crocodile was terribly strong.

The corpse of a boy floated past the ship; a monstrous crocodile rushed at it with the speed of a greyhound, caught it and shook it, as a terrier dog does a rat. Others dashed at the prey, each with his powerful tail causing the water to churn and froth, as he furiously tore off a piece. In a few seconds it was all gone. The sight was frightful to behold. The Shire swarmed with crocodiles; we counted sixty-seven of these repulsive reptiles on a single bank, but they are not as fierce as they are in some rivers. "Crocodiles," says Captain Tuckey, "are so plentiful in the Congo, near the rapids, and so frequently carry off the women, who at daylight go down to the river for water, that, while they are filling their calabashes, one of the party is usually employed in throwing large stones into the water outside." Here, either a calabash on a long pole is used in drawing water, or a fence is planted. The natives eat the crocodile, but to us the idea of tasting the musky-scented, fishy-looking flesh carried the idea of cannibalism. Humboldt remarks, that in South America the alligators of some rivers are more dangerous than in others. Alligators differ from crocodiles in the fourth or canine tooth going into a hole or socket in the upper jaw, while, in the crocodile it fits into a notch. The forefoot of the crocodile has five toes not webbed, the hindfoot has four toes which are webbed; in the alligator the web is altogether wanting. They are so much alike that they would no doubt breed together.

One of the crocodiles which was shot had a piece snapped off the end of his tail, another had lost a forefoot in fighting; we saw actual leeches between the teeth, such as are mentioned by Herodotus, but we never witnessed the plover picking them out. Their greater fierceness in one part of the country than another is doubtless owing to a scarcity of fish; in fact, Captain Tuckey says, of that part of the Congo, mentioned above, "There are no fish here but catfish," and we found, that the lake crocodiles, living in clear water, and with plenty of fish, scarcely ever attacked man. The Shire teems with fish of many different kinds. The only time, as already remarked, when its crocodiles are particularly to be dreaded, is when the river is in flood. Then the fish are driven from their usual haunts, and no game comes down to the river to drink, water being abundant in pools inland. Hunger now impels the crocodile to lie in wait for the women who come to draw water, and on the Zambesi numbers are carried off every year. The danger is not so great at other seasons; though it is never safe to bathe, or to stoop to drink, where one cannot see the bottom, especially in the evening. One of the Makololo ran down in the dusk to the river; and, as he was busy tossing the water to his mouth with his hand, in the manner peculiar to the natives, a crocodile rose suddenly from the bottom, and caught him by the hand. The limb of a tree was fortunately within reach, and he had presence of mind to lay hold of it. Both tugged and pulled; the crocodile for his dinner, and the man for dear life. For a time, it appeared doubtful whether a dinner or a life was to be sacrificed; but the man held on, and the monster let the hand go, leaving the deep marks of his ugly teeth in it.

During our detention, in expectation of the permanent rise of the river in March, Dr. Kirk and Mr. C. Livingstone collected numbers of the wading-birds of the marshes—and made pleasant additions to our salted provisions, in geese, ducks, and hippopotamus flesh. One of the comb or knob-nosed geese, on being strangled in order to have its skin preserved without injury, continued to breathe audibly by the broken humerus, or wing-bone, and other means had to be adopted to put it out of pain. This was as if a man on the gallows were to continue to breathe by a broken armbone, and afforded us an illustration of the fact, that in birds, the vital air penetrates every part of the interior of their bodies. The breath passes through and round about the lungs—bathes the surfaces of the viscera, and enters the cavities of the bones; it even penetrates into some spaces between the muscles of the neck—and thus not only is the most perfect oxygenation of the blood secured, but, the temperature of the blood being very high, the air in every part is rarefied, and the great lightness and vigour provided for, that the habits of birds require. Several birds were found by Dr. Kirk, to have marrow in the tibiæ, though these bones are generally described as hollow.

During the period of our detention on the shallow part of the river in March, Mr. Thornton came up to us from

Shupanga: he had, as before narrated, left the expedition in 1859, and joined Baron van der Decken, in the journey to Kilimanjaro, when, by an ascent of the mountain to the height of 8000 feet, it was first proved to be covered with perpetual snow, and the previous information respecting it, given by the Church of England Missionaries, Krapf and Rebman, confirmed. It is now well known that the Baron subsequently ascended the Kilimanjaro to 14,000 feet, and ascertained its highest peak to be at least 20,000 feet above the sea. Mr Thornton made the map of the first journey, at Shupanga, from materials collected when with the Baron; and when that work was accomplished, followed us. He was then directed to examine geologically, the Cataract district, but not to expose himself to contact with the Ajawa until the feelings of that tribe should be ascertained.

The members of Bishop Mackenzie's party had, on the loss of their head, fled from Magomero on the highlands, down to Chibisa's, in the low-lying Shire Valley; and Thornton, finding them suffering from want of animal food, kindly volunteered to go across thence to Tette, and bring a supply of goats and sheep. We were not aware of this step, to which the generosity of his nature prompted him, till two days after he had started. In addition to securing supplies for the Universities' Mission, he brought some for the Expedition, and took bearings, by which he hoped to connect his former work at Tette with the mountains in the Shire district. The toil of this journey was too much for his strength, as with the addition of great scarcity of water, it had been for that of Dr. Kirk and Rae, and he returned in a sadly haggard and exhausted condition; diarrhœa supervened, and that ended in dysentery and fever, which terminated fatally on the 21st of April, 1863. He received the unremitting attentions of Dr. Kirk, and Dr. Meller, surgeon of the Pioneer, during the fortnight of his illness; and as he had suffered very little from fever, or any other disease, in Africa, we had entertained strong hopes that his youth and unimpaired constitution would have carried him through. During the night of the 20th, his mind wandered so much, that we could not ascertain his last wishes; and on the morning of the 21st, to our great sorrow, he died. He was buried on the 22nd, near a large tree on the right bank of the Shire, about five hundred yards from the lowest of the Murchison Cataracts—and close to a rivulet, at which the Lady Nyassa and Pioneer lay.

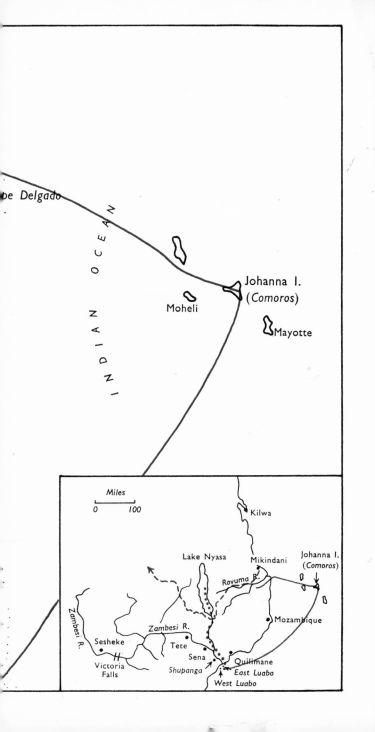

be Delgado

INDIAN OCEAN

Johanna I.
(Comoros)

Moheli

Mayotte

Miles

0   100

Kilwa

Lake Nyasa

Mikindani

Johanna I.
(Comoros)

Rovuma R.

Zambesi R.

Mozambique

Seseke

Zambesi R.

Tete

Sena

Quilimane

Victoria
Falls

Shupanga

East Luabo

West Luabo

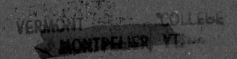